The Church Year at Home

The Church Year at Home

*A Practical Guide for Using the Church
Calendar to Frame Time with Our Kids*

CHRISTINE E. CURLEY

RESOURCE *Publications* • Eugene, Oregon

THE CHURCH YEAR AT HOME
A Practical Guide for Using the Church Calendar to Frame Time with Our Kids

Resource Publications
An Imprint of Wipf and Stock Publishers
199 W. 8th Ave., Suite 3
Eugene, OR 97401

www.wipfandstock.com

PAPERBACK ISBN: 978-1-6667-0904-9
HARDCOVER ISBN: 978-1-6667-0905-6
EBOOK ISBN: 978-1-6667-0906-3

07/27/21

To my five kiddos, Maddie, Mark, Kevin, Evie, and Cassie.
Thanks for inspiring me to seek after God to raise you.

Contents

Introduction   ix

1   Advent   1

2   Christmas   9

3   Epiphany   14

4   Ordinary Time: The Season after Epiphany and the
    Season after Pentecost   18

5   Fat Tuesday, Ash Wednesday, and Lent   27

6   Easter and the Easter Season   49

7   Ascension and Pentecost   60

8   Reformation Day, All Saints Day, and Christ the King   66

Conclusion   71

Bibliography   73

Introduction

We all have routines and rhythms. Most of us get up around the same time each day, eat a similar breakfast as the day before, go to work or school, eat, sleep. Routines and rhythms help us to feel secure in our lives. They are comfortable and reassuring. The same is true for yearly or seasonal rhythms. It is August while I am writing this, and school is starting all around the country. People are taking first day of school pictures, and the stores have school supplies in the aisles. Soon, of course, it will turn to Halloween candy and costumes, only to give way to a cursory nod to Thanksgiving, and then of course Christmas.

The rhythm of the year is no less true for the church. Each new season brings a new focus, and a new beginning. It allows for a rhythm in our spiritual lives. Instead of following the seasons and changes of the world around us, the church year allows us to enter into a new story—the story of Jesus. It gives shape to our rhythms in such a way as to be a spiritual pilgrimage. As Robert Webber explains in his 1997 book, *Worship is a Verb: Eight Principles to Transforming Worship*, the calendar's, "purpose is to relive the life of Christ, to walk in the footsteps of Jesus, to experience what Jesus experienced, to identify with his earthly life, and through that experience, to grow spiritually." I now enter not into the story of culture, but rather Christ's. Our days have structure and new meaning through him.

The rhythms and routines of the church year are not meant to be a weight that forces you to do something. Rather, they act as anchors in the face of a tumultuous sea. We have so many things coming at us all the time. We have sports practices, and art stuff, and school, and getting food on the table. We want to be able to say yes to our kids' desires. We want to say yes to the needs of the church and the community. We want to say yes to all the fun activities. The reality is we cannot do everything we want to do. We need some boundaries. So often we don't want to be the one who says no we can't do something because it is just too much—too much time away from the family, too much expense, too much anything. I am guilty of this myself. But, we can say no. For example, if something is not in the budget one month, you simply can't buy it. I think we need to see our time that way, too. If something conflicts on a consistent basis with our time with the Lord, we need to say no. If something takes away from our responsibility of raising our children to be disciples of Jesus, then we need to rethink our priorities. Further, most of us need shape and structure to our time with the Lord in order to make the most of it. Our routines set parameters and they release us to say yes to the great, instead of being bogged down with the ok. Our discipline to follow God's calendar combats exhaustion and stress, because as we shall see, often times when the world around us demands that we pay attention to all its shiny objects, the church's calendar invites us to slow down and reorient our attentions.

This book is not about trying to celebrate every single Christian holiday each year. Nor is it about following the lectionary. Instead, this is meant to be a tool to help you and your family invite Jesus into your daily lives. As Lauren Winner writes in the forward to Bobby Gross's 2009 *Living the Christian Year: Time to Inhabit the Story of God*, "I want the Christian story to shape everything I do, even how I reckon time." I find the seasons of the year offer a way to center not only myself, but also my children on looking at Jesus—who he is, what he did, and then how we are to live. I think that much to our discredit, many in the Protestant traditions have shuffled off so much of what Rome preserved for us in the effort to reform the church, that we lost some of daily and seasonal routines that help us to keep our eyes on Jesus. What I hope to offer are simple ways to give shape to your annual spiritual rhythm.

When God called Israel and made them his people, he set them apart in many different ways, from dress, to food, to how they worshipped. Many of the things that God commanded the Jews to do were for their own good. The rules and routines constantly placed God first, from their rising to their going to sleep. Because of their relationship with God, they dressed differently from the nations around them. Because they loved God, their days looked different, and they took one day each week to fully rest and worship God. They ate only certain foods. All of these things acted as markers to remind them that God is God, and they are not, and that they were set apart.

We as the church are called to be set apart. This means that how we conduct our lives should not just be normal plus God. They should be infused with God. Christians in America have lost that feeling of being distinctive. So much of how we act does not necessarily appear any different from the rest of the world. Many of us, myself included, do not dress radically different than the rest of the culture. Nor do our holidays stand in contrast to secular society. A Christian Christmas and a secular Christmas will probably look very similar from the outside. The same is true for Easter. What I hope to offer is to give you and your family an opportunity to recapture a Christo-centric view of our year.

This book is meant to be a resource to find other resources. There is so much available today it can seem overwhelming. I want to give you a few pointers to help you on your way, and in the end, you can find what works for your family. This book is not meant to make you feel guilty about what you are or are not doing. I offer a look at some of the major seasons of the church year, and how you can use them in your family's spiritual walk. I outline some of the things that my family has done. Don't feel like your life has to look like ours—it won't, and that is the way it should be. I think now more than ever we need to be proactive and disciplined to make new disciples, mainly our children. As I have been reminded recently, God calls families as the primary crucible for faith. As parents, God charges us with teaching our children who he is, and what he has done for us, and further how our lives should be changed to reflect that. We constantly form and reform our lives so as not to be pulled under by the influence of the surrounding culture.

I have laid out this book to cover the main Christian seasons starting with Advent, the beginning of the church year. I present a brief history and theology of each season, followed by some ideas of how to incorporate it into your life. Finally, I list some resources that I have found helpful with some comments about them. I include crafts and activities as well as Bible passages. My kids always want to do crafts and activities. I have to admit, creating crafts is not my strong suit, but I am capable of finding them. I am also not the craftiest person, so usually my rationale for whether I will do a craft is if it is simple, and I have the supplies mostly on hand. Further, I find *Pinterest* overwhelming, and therefore all the websites I have included are not *Pinterest*. And remember, this is not something that is just another item on your to-do list. My prayer is that this helps you to start a new journey with your family to delve into the Scriptures, and therefore fall deeper in love with God. Before you start any of these ideas, place it before God and see if he is directing you in this way.

1

Advent

HISTORY AND THEOLOGY

There are plenty of new year's throughout the 365 days it takes to orbit the sun. We have the Western New Year celebrated 1 January. The Chinese New Year, based upon the lunar calendar, occurs in either January or February. There are other new year's as well, such as the new school year, which starts in the fall, as well as birthdays and anniversaries. For the church, the calendar starts with Advent 1, which is the fourth Sunday before Christmas. This is usually the Sunday after Thanksgiving and can vary between 27 November and 3 December. In our culture today, that usually coincides with what is known as the Christmas season—the time for parties, pageants, parades, Santa, and who can forget, presents!

Advent is a season of preparation. The word advent means a beginning, or something new. For Christians, we recognize that Jesus' birth marked a change in God's relationship with us. He started something new. The Incarnation is a powerful message that God is among us. No longer content to be at arms' distance, Jesus chose to live with us, and to start his life with us as a baby. Getting ready to welcome a new baby takes a lot of work. Most parents spend many waking hours thinking and preparing for this new bundle of joy. At

Christmas we are not simply welcoming a baby, but the Son of God. This calls for some serious planning!

Advent has a double focus. Not only do we prepare to celebrate Jesus' birth, but we also anticipate his second coming. As we rejoice in his birth, we also keep watch for the fulfillment of prophecies. We recognize we all yearn for God to deliver justice in our world and make all things right. As the days become darker, we look to Jesus to bring light to the world once again, and we ask ourselves how we can prepare for such an occasion.

As a season of preparation, Advent evolved throughout the centuries. As early as the mid-fourth century the church introduced a preparation period for Epiphany, a day marked in the Eastern Church for baptisms. As the years progressed more churches engaged in a four- or five-week penitential season before Christmas. By the middle ages we see the common four-week schedule that we see today.

If we are honest with ourselves, the day after Christmas is kind of a let-down. Even Christmas evening is anti-climactic. All the build-up and planning, and then it is all over. Presents are strewn all over the floor. We are stuffed, and if we are honest, sometimes a bit bored. I find that this feeling is heightened when I do not participate in Advent. Christmas is just one more celebration in a whole month of celebrations, and it does not feel special. I think we wonder if it was all worth it? When we can focus more clearly on Jesus and his Incarnation and birth, we can enter into a more joyous celebration.

Much of the Christian walk is waiting on God's timing. This is a hard thing to do. Of course we want whatever we want now. It would be easier and require a whole lot less faith. When we delay the pleasure of Christmas, it gives us some of the training we need to wait upon the Lord in the bigger things in life and helps to instill the same discipline for our children.

HOW CAN I GET STARTED?

The question then becomes, what should Advent look like? What do we do when we prepare? How do we make the most of the time, and juggle everything that we want to do? How do we put Jesus first in this season? When we look at what we are prioritizing, is it Jesus, or other things?

When you get ready to host a guest, what do you do? Well, if you are like my family, we talk about it a lot. My kids get excited about all the fun things we will do when someone special is here. As the parent, I also think about all the chores I need to do. I think about all the cleaning that needs to happen and how to rearrange rooms and people if necessary. Then, of course there is the meal planning. The day our expected guests are to arrive we always hurry to get all the extras finished. It is always the case that I think, 'Oh, I have two more things to do," and then I look into a room and see a whole new mess and realize I have about six more things to do. I often feel the same way about the month of December. We have extra cleaning, extra meal planning, extra events, extra everything. And when we think that we have one or two more things to do, we look into another room and recognize the whole pile of presents we still need to wrap, and the bathroom needs to be cleaned. The list goes on.

So how can we approach our spiritual preparation without feeling the same way? We still need to ask ourselves, what do we want to accomplish? What are the most important things we want to do? How can we make God the center of this season and not merely an add-on? How can we get our kids involved? If we don't have a game plan, it simply won't happen. There have been times when my family has wanted to do a certain activity, or participate in something special for the season, but if we don't sit down and decide when and how this will happen, it most certainly will not happen. We end up disappointed.

When we prepare spiritually, we are cleaning. We are stripping down to the basics, paring away clutter in our spiritual lives. Historically, Advent was a penitential season in order to fully participate in the joy of Christmas. As a penitential season, people fasted. Some people fasted and then used the money they saved to bless a family that was poor with food for Christmas. I know fasting during this time of year is not very popular. I know fasting in general is not very popular, but as a spiritual discipline it allows us to depend on God for our needs. Fasting is not my favorite spiritual discipline, but I have found that when I approach it faithfully, God is faithful, too. We fast because God calls us to fast.

Fasting makes space for God. It is not meant to be a weight loss system. The point of fasting, whether it be a meal once a week, or for a day once a week, is to make time for God. Instead of eating during that time, you spend those minutes in prayer and study. When we hunger for food, we are reminded of our true hunger for God. It gives God room to work. It gives him time. It makes us humble and forces us to realize our dependence on him. But remember what Jesus told us about how to act when we fast: don't tell everyone and show how miserable you are. Just do it. Do it quietly unto God. Give him the ability to clean out your house in order that you are ready to welcome the Spirit.

While many people immediately think of food to fast, it need not be the thing you choose. In our day of technology, putting down your phone for a portion of the day, or abstaining from TV (and I would include all forms, Hulu, Netflix, etc.), or anything else that might distract you from spending time with God is a good place to start. As the parent in the family, we model by our actions more than our words, so even if our children are too young to fast, they can see how our actions change during the Advent season.

I know that the above portion is more geared to the adults in the family, but when your children are ready, introduce the concept of fasting. Growing up in the Anglican tradition, having a Lenten discipline, for example was commonplace. I remember fasting from dessert as early as middle school. We may decide for our children a certain fast, such as from electronic devices on a certain night of the week so the family can spend time reading the Bible or doing an Advent activity together. As the parent, you decide what you will fix for dinner. You may decide that you will not have meat for dinner one day a week, or you will have a simple and cheap meal, in order to give that money to others. When asked why the family has made such changes, start a conversation about the season.

Discuss with your children what they want to do. I am not a Grinch, imposing a zero-Christmas policy on my family. We have traditions we like to do each year before Christmas, such as the local Christmas parade, looking at lights, and one Christmas party. We prioritize these outings, and say no to others. Just as we need to consider fasting from food, we may need to fast from certain events or parties. It may be that it is just one too many, or we know that a particular party may not be God honoring. We have the freedom to say no, and recognize that God calls us not to everything, but to the best.

Beyond this, what will a typical day in Advent look like? How may it differ from any other day? Well, let me tell you what my family does. Since we homeschool, we have a bit more flexibility in our schedule, but even if your kids are in school, you can still make some simple changes. We usually have a Bible portion in our day. We spend this time doing our Advent craft. This usually takes longer than our typical Bible study, but that is ok. Usually by this time in the year, everyone needs a little break anyway. My favorite Advent resource is *The Truth in the Tinsel*, by Amanda White We have used it for many years. Every day there is a Scripture reading, a simple (yes, it is simple with things you have around the house for the most part or that can be substituted) craft, and questions and discussion ideas. Currently my kids are nine, seven, four, two, and six months. The older two complete the crafts, the four-year-old does most, but not all the crafts, and the two-year-old usually just scribbles. Typically, we do this in the morning.

We also observe Advent at the dinner table. After we finish eating, and the dishes have (mostly) been cleared, we bring out our candles and Advent wreath. Yes, you can light candles even with small children. It is not for a long time, and they can learn to be careful of the flame. Further, they love it. We have a very simple Advent wreath. It is about six inches wide, and I place it, along with two-inch-tall candles on a small plate. It is not overly complicated, nor does it take up much room on our small table.

We light the Advent candles and read from an Advent calendar I got years ago before I was even married. It is a collection of small board books that can be used as ornaments. Each book has only a few lines about some aspect of the Christmas story. It takes a minute or two to read. I will admit, it makes my very Pentecostal husband cringe at times because she names the wise men the traditional names: Casper, Balthazar, and Melchior. Clearly, an extrabiblical reading. One year we added "Kids Read Truth Advent Cards," which have a Scripture reading, and then three questions you can ask. This year we used the She Reads Truth Scripture pop-out ornaments; each had a verse written on it which we read and then added it to the tree. We like to sing an Advent hymn. This I am a bit strict on. We try to not sing Christmas carols until Christmas. Sometimes we talk about what we have read, sometimes we just hold the kids back long enough so that the person whose turn it is to blow out the candles actually gets their turn. Life with five is chaotic and wonderful. What I am trying to say is, don't think my children sit nicely with their hands folded in their laps nodding through the story, and then politely asking to blow out the candles. Many nights it is sheer pandemonium, but we do it, and they love it. They expect it during Advent, and getting ready for Christmas would not be the same without it.

Now, let me say something about Advent wreaths. These can be very simple. The tradition is to have an evergreen wreath with four candles along the outside and one white candle in the middle as the Christ candle. As I already mentioned, Advent is a penitential season, so traditionally the church lights three purple candles and one pink candle. Recently some churches moved to using three blue candles and one pink candle to distinguish Advent from Lent. Either way, you follow the same routine. Each Sunday you light one more candle, blue, blue, pink, blue, and each week has a different theme. The themes are not set in stone. Most people follow the themes hope, peace, joy, love, but there are other ones such as prophecy, promise, fulfillment, faith. In Advent there is a lightening part way through. The third Sunday is almost always joy since we know that joy is coming through the darkness, and that is why one of the candles is pink. The final central white candle is lit on Christmas. In essence, it is a countdown calendar to prepare us and to remind us of what is to come.

Another simple thing you can do during the Advent and Christmas season is set up a manger. This need not be a really expensive manger set. I remember playing with our manger set as a kid. I set up all the people, but they would not be in the manger when I first set it up, instead, they traveled. Each day during Advent, I moved them closer until finally they reached the manger on Christmas Eve with the baby Jesus hidden behind it, only to make his appearance after we celebrated in church. I admit I have hesitated to introduce a manger with my kids. The foremost reason is that they break things. My two-year-old is a force unto herself. We do, however, have a Fisher-Price Nativity set my grandmother gave to my oldest daughter when she was one. It only comes out during Advent and Christmas. They are able to play with the different people on their own time. A manger is a useful visual and tactile tool for the Christmas and Advent season. If your Advent discipline talks about individual people, such as Mary or Joseph, have your kids hold them and talk about them.

RESOURCES

Croll, Carolyn. *The Story of Christmas: Storybook set and Advent Calendar*. New York: Workman, 2008. If you look it up on Amazon it has mixed reviews. We use it because it gives the Christmas story in bit-sized chunks, and the books are cute. However, I will warn you that there is definitely extra-biblical information. It includes the traditional names of the three Wise Men. Further, because she spaces it out over twenty-four days, she adds details about the journey and such. I would not use this as your sole Advent curriculum, but if you use it in addition to something else, then I think it is a good tool.

Fischer, Melissa. *Fisch Tale Design*. https://www.etsy.com/shop/fischtaledesigns?ref=simple-shop-header-name&listing_id=685759537. This is an Etsy shop that sells paper crafts you can print at home. She has a paper puppet Nativity scene which is a download. This is a good alternative if you cannot afford a manager, or don't want to invest in one with young kids.

Kids Read Truth Advent Cards. This is available from She Reads Truth at https://www.shopshereadstruth.com/collections/kids-read-truth. They direct you to a Scripture reading, and then they have three questions, each one geared to different age groups. This is a straightforward and simple way to bring the family into the Advent season.

White, Amanda. *The Truth in the Tinsel: An Advent Experience for Little Hands.* Amanda White, 2011. This is my favorite Advent devotional for families. This is an eBook available at https://truthinthetinsel.com/shop/. The basic book is $10. Each day has a Scripture reading, followed by a very simple craft, and then she has questions and discussion ideas. She has alternative schedules if you cannot commit to every day.

2

Christmas

HISTORY AND THEOLOGY

Christmas celebrates Jesus' birth. The Incarnation, or God becoming flesh is a supernatural feat. John tells us that "The Word became flesh, and dwelt among us." (John 1:14 NKJ) What an incredible thing our God has done. This is a day that is clearly a celebration. Anytime a baby is born it is cause to celebrate, but the Son of God? This requires extra festivities! Jesus took on all of our weaknesses. He lived in a fragile mortal body. He lived with our smells and our sins. He saw all the things we do right and wrong, and he loved us through it all. Yet, he did not come into this world in a grand palace, but rather in a humble stable. He humbled himself for us. This is incredible.

The celebration of Christmas has had many ups and downs. Bruce David Forbes in his 2007 book, *Christmas: A Candid History* argues that from the beginning of celebrating Christmas, it was "a combination of winter cultural party and Christian observance." There have been periods in Christian history in which it was strictly banned such as under the Puritan rule in England in the seventeenth century. Other times it was a raucous event marked by extreme partying (which is what led it to being banned by the Puritans). Honestly, its placement in December does not line up with when most scholars believe Jesus was born. However, by about the mid-fourth century we have evidence that the early Christian church celebrated some form of Christmas around mid-December or early January. It sometimes overlapped with Epiphany. The cultural winter holidays, and many cultures have one, in which people celebrate the shortest day of the year, coincided with the imagery of what Jesus did. Jesus, the Light of the World, entered the darkened world. He brings hope and life when we only see darkness and death.

In the church year Christmas is not a one-day event, instead Christmas lasts for twelve days. After all the preparation you really get to enjoy it. This does not mean you need to plan and prepare a feast for twelve days. After all the hustle and bustle of cleaning, and baking, and presents, take time to simply enjoy it all. So, yes, indulge in your favorite desserts and other tasty bites. Take time to do all the things you have been putting off because, let's face it, December is a busy time of year.

HOW CAN I GET STARTED?

After roughly a month of preparation, now is the time for celebration! Now we enjoy the fruits of our labors. I am sure that your family has many traditions, and I think that they are probably just right for your family. You may be thinking, how can I incorporate faith into Christmas? Or how can I not get bogged down in all the things we have to do to enjoy Christmas? I know this can be hard. Christians walk a fine line of celebrating the Christian Christmas and the cultural Christmas, since the cultural winter holiday celebrations inundate almost all aspects of life come December. What should Christmas day and the following twelve days look like? These are good questions and can be hard to answer if your extended family are not practicing Christians but still celebrate Christmas.

First of all, go to church. I know that some churches have moved away from having Christmas services. This is a detriment to everyone. Christmas is one of the few times of the year that non-Christians will darken the door of a church. But, even more than that, Christians should spend a holy day in church surrounded by other believers. If we aim to make faith and worship a central part of our lives, then corporate worship needs to be a component of this plan. What better way to celebrate Jesus' birth, than to gather with believers, rehearse the Christmas story, sing our favorite Christmas carols, and join in fellowship together?

To be honest, my favorite part of Christmas is the Christmas Eve service. I love going to church when it is dark and cold, and yet light shines inside the cozy church. At the end of the service, we light candles and sing Silent Night. Throughout the service we sing lots of good Christmas carols. Singing the same hymns every year, hearing the Scripture, being in church, these make it a celebration. It is a special time of worship, meant to remind us of the extraordinary work God did so many years ago, but also what he continues to do today in our lives.

Before kids, I always went to the midnight service. It is more solemn, and there is something special about going to church so late at night. If you have older kids who can handle staying up late, I suggest going to this service. They feel like they are doing something extra special, and who doesn't want to stay up late on Christmas? Instead of waiting for Santa, we are keeping watch for the Christ child. I remember going as a teen, and it was certainly something I looked forward to. It had such a different feel from the normal church services—excitement and expectation, along with darkness and light. If your home church does not offer this service, you may try a different church just for the evening.

Now that we have five young kids, the idea of a midnight service is incomprehensible—they simply would not be able to function, and it would be miserable. The church where we go for Christmas has a family service usually around 4:30 or 5:00 in the afternoon. This is perfect for us. Geared toward children, the service includes the children by helping the pastor arrange the manger. They are full participants in the work of worship. The kids also know that once we have gone to church, then it is officially Christmas.

After the service we come home and have a meal. Since we have celebrated Christmas through worship, we allow our kids to open up their Christmas presents from us. Our kids receive simple presents on Christmas to draw their attention to the celebration of

Jesus' birth. We give our kids Christmas boxes. Inside are new jammies, a homemade pillowcase, a photobook from the past year, a book, sometimes a small toy or socks, and a new movie. For a while we tried to get Christmas movies, but now we just try to choose wholesome or Christian movies. The kids change into their new jammies, and I pop popcorn. They either watch one of their new movies or *The Promise*, a computer animated musical about the birth of Jesus, which follows the Bible fairly closely. Even if we do not watch *The Promise* on Christmas Eve, we do watch it at some point during Christmas.

By having a church centric Christmas Eve, I feel more comfortable about having a more culturally focused Christmas Day. We gather at my parents' house along with other family members. We open presents, we have a big meal, and we hang out together.

I know that everyone's Christmas looks different. Some people have family close by and will visit with them. Others travel long distances. Some people stay at home. Some people have very time-honored traditions, others do not. For me, after Christmas morning and the preparation for Christmas dinner (usually mid-afternoon for us), there doesn't seem to be much to do. The cultural Christmas can be rather disheartening after the initial excitement wears off.

After the month of December and Christmas itself, the idea of celebrating for twelve more days may seem to be too much. Keep in mind a few things. One, if you follow the discipline of Advent, then you have not been celebrating Christmas for the past month, so you have celebrating left in you. Two, do not feel pressured to have a *Pinterest* worthy Christmas day every day for the next twelve days. It can be something simple, like planning to make your children's favorite snacks for a few days. Make special crafts or ornaments. Bake some of the things you did not get a chance to make. Have a game night. Watch special movies that you only view during the Christmas season.

Choose a few days during this time to do something special with your family. Go ice skating, sledding, or walking in your neighborhood to see the lights. Instead of spending as much money on toys for your kids for Christmas morning, spend some of that money on a special treat. For example, my daughter always wants to paint pottery when we visit my parents for Christmas, and my son likes to go to a local model train display. Usually they get to do these things just one-on-one with either myself or my husband. In other words, you can probably integrate some of the things you already do. Perhaps some things you would normally do before Christmas can be moved to after Christmas to make this time more special.

RESOURCES

Mitchell, Alison. *The Christmas Promise.* Charlotte: The Good Book Company, 2014. In her usual fashion, Mitchell gives a lighthearted, but Gospel centered retelling of the Christmas story. The pictures are wonderful, and all my kids love this book. You can also purchase a coloring book that goes with it.

Myers, Raechel, Melanie Rainer, Amanda Bible Williams. *This is the Christmas Story: A Kids Read Truth Story and Scripture Book.* Nashville: Kids Read Truth, 2017. This book gives the Christmas story in bright pictures. It also offers Scripture passages indicating how Jesus fulfilled a promise or prophecy.

Shaffer, Todd, dir. *The Promise.* 2013; Montreal, QC: Glorious Films. DVD. This is a delightful movie, about 45 minutes long. As I said, it is a musical, and the kids love it. It follows the Christmas story well.

3

Epiphany

HISTORY AND THEOLOGY

When we think of an epiphany, we often envision a sudden and somewhat unexpected inspiration like a light bulb coming on. Whereas Advent is an enduring expectation of something new about to happen, Epiphany is unforeseen and shorter. Today Epiphany recognizes the visit of the three kings and the church celebrates on 6 January. The visit from the magi signals that Jesus' ministry, while initially directed to the Jews, ultimately encompasses the whole world. These outsiders recognized Jesus as far more than simply a prophet or teacher, they came to worship him.

Epiphany traditionally displays Jesus' divinity. Some churches celebrate Jesus' baptism in the Jordan River on 6 January or soon afterward. In the Eastern Church it is a day for baptisms. It is also a day for blessings. Some churches offer blessed chalk to take to your home and write 20+C+M+B+the last two digits of the year above the door. (CMB stands for the Latin for *Christus mansionem benedicat*, Christ bless this house). In some ways Epiphany and the season after it is a bit of a hodge-podge, with different traditions coming together and the modern church trying to offer some form of coherent practice.

Some people in the early church celebrated Christmas on 6 January, but about the fourth or fifth century in the West we see a division between Christmas and Epiphany. Local churches determined when they observed the holiday, and so different parts of the world migrated to this pattern at different times. Epiphany also marks the end of the Christmas season. After Epiphany we will move into Ordinary Time.

HOW CAN I GET STARTED?

Epiphany is an often-overlooked holiday, but it can still be a day that we look to Jesus and remember once again the gift he gave in becoming a human. My kids look forward to the day each year because they know it is a mini holiday. We will have a fun breakfast, and of course presents, followed by a nice dinner at night. We finish watching our Christmas movies, before packing them away for another year. Since we homeschool, we do not have school that day. It is our last day of the Christmas holiday, and the kids enjoy every minute of it.

I read or tell the story of the magi coming to Jesus on Epiphany. Sometimes we use the manger if we have the pieces readily available. There are several books about the wise men that you can find in the resource section. Sometimes we read one of those, and sometimes we simply read the Bible. Spend time talking about the gifts the wise men brought. I remember someone gave me a small bit of frankincense and myrrh when I was about seven or eight. I remember looking at them and keeping them in a small treasure box that I had. If you can get ahold of either of these, it would be instructive for your children. Or, in these days of essential oils, you could get these oils and have your children smell them.

An easy way to celebrate Epiphany with kids is to give small gifts. I know that the idea of presents at this point might seem overwhelming, but hear me out. The magi came bearing gifts, so it is not too far off base to want to do the same. It also allows for some anticipation after Christmas that something more is coming. Epiphany need not be a second Christmas. It is more of a last hurrah before Ordinary Time settles in. I remember when I was growing up, I left my shoes outside my bedroom door, and in the morning there would be a few pieces of candy in them. Children in Spain and Mexico still do this. Since we celebrate Christmas with my parents, my kids still want to have stockings of their own, so on Epiphany I fill their stockings. I do not stuff them. I put a favorite candy bar in them, maybe some socks or school supplies if they need them, or maybe some toothpaste. In other words, it is nothing fancy or extravagant, rather a fun surprise on the day.

Food is another important factor in any holiday. As you build your traditions, think about what foods you may want to serve each year. For our family, any holiday or birthday calls for cinnamon rolls for breakfast. When we have cinnamon rolls, the kids know that this is a special day. There are a few traditional foods for Epiphany. Hot apple cider is a traditional drink for Epiphany in England. Some people, especially French or Spanish, will have King Cake. The cake varies per region, but it is often colored and has something hidden inside it to represent baby Jesus. My kids are not big fans of King Cake, so we have donuts instead.

If your family enjoys crafts and activities, here are some ideas. Make crowns. These can be simple construction paper crowns that your kids color, or if you have the time and desire, go all out. Make a wonderful crown. Pretend you are the magi coming to see Jesus. What would it feel like? Remind your children once again that Jesus is the true king. Since the magi followed a star, do activities that feature stars. Decorate your home with stars your children make as you take down the other Christmas decorations. If it is not too cold, go outside and gaze at the stars.

Finally, I know that everyone has different schedules for when they decorate for Christmas. Some people eagerly unpack boxes starting in November or just after Thanksgiving, while others wait closer to Christmas. And then, the reverse is true for putting away all the Christmas stuff—some people readily take it down the day after Christmas, and others keep it up half the year. Celebrating Epiphany gives us a deliberate end point to the Christmas season and also an end point for decorations. As part of the family's spiritual discipline, take down the decorations the day after Epiphany, since the feasting season has now come to an end.

RESOURCES

Alavedra, Joan. *They Followed a Bright Star*. New York: Putnam Juvenile, 1994. This book is now out of print, but you can find it relatively cheaply online. While we hear about what the shepherds did on the night of Jesus' birth, this imagines how others followed the star and were faithful in what God called them to do when Jesus was born.

Park, Linda Sue. *The Third Gift*. New York: Clarion, 2011. This book imagines the day a first century myrrh finder and his father found the myrrh the wise men took to Jesus. It goes through how they find myrrh, and then how they sell it to the three wise men. It is a sweet book about the costliness of the gifts given to Jesus.

Spirin, Gennady. *We Three Kings*. New York: Atheneum Books for Young Readers, 2007. This book uses the hymn as its text, and Spirin has made striking pictures to illustrate it.

4

Ordinary Time

The Season after Epiphany and the Season after Pentecost

HISTORY AND THEOLOGY

There are two major seasons in the church calendar which are called Ordinary Time. The first one, the Season after Epiphany, lasts from Epiphany until Ash Wednesday, and the second one, the Season after Pentecost, stretches from Pentecost until Advent. The church spends the majority of the year in these two seasons. The term Ordinary Time comes from the fact that the weeks are numbered, that is ordered. While this season represents the ordinary time of our lives, that does not mean God ceases to do extraordinary things. God moves in the ordinary times of our lives, not only in the holidays and exciting times. Plodding through the daily grind shapes us and makes us. Putting one foot in front of the other even when it is not exciting or fun makes us disciples of Christ. Paul speaks to this type of training in First Corinthians 9:24–27 when he exhorts his listeners to work diligently.

While we do not necessarily have any indication of these seasons from the early church, by the Middle Ages we see these designations. However, it stands to reason that for most Christians throughout the centuries, Ordinary Time, whether it was called that or not, is the way life works most of the time. So, use this time to further embed yourself in God's story. This is an opportune time to focus on our daily walk with Christ. You may want to try something new or continue in a time-tested discipline. Either way, the majority of the year is meant for us to be shaped by God's crucible of life and discipleship.

HOW CAN I GET STARTED?

Ordinary Time presents the opportunity to assess our spiritual life. While not always comfortable, analyzing our walk with Jesus and being open to acknowledging our blind spots not only humbles us, but strengthens us. Look for areas of weakness that need bolstering. Search out your areas of strength in which you delight in what God is teaching you. Look at your calendar and judge the amount of space you have to grow in your walk with God. If every day is completely full, consider chopping some activities. Dare to try something new.

My younger children often have a hard time remembering what the day is, and what activities we are doing that day. So, for example, my kids constantly ask, "Are we going to church today?" or "Do we go to the library today?" Keeping track of our days can be hard. I finally decided to print out a calendar for the kids and mark on them our special activities. This does not prevent the two-year-old from still asking consistently throughout the day if we are going to church. It does help the older kids to recognize the rhythms of our weeks.

By having a rhythm to our days and our weeks and months, it helps our children understand time. They gain an appreciation for the rhythm of daily, weekly, monthly, and yearly tasks. They can order their lives. By regulating our lives around the church's calendar, we orient our children to put God and his rhythms first. God shows himself in all aspects of our lives, not merely when we are at church or studying the Bible, but in all our routines as well. By following the church's calendar, it allows us to see God even in the mundane and the ordinary because God works in all things.

What does this look like? This will look different for each family. We have to juggle our own spiritual disciplines and those of our family as well. Our kids watch us in all things, so demonstrate for them the importance of spending time in the Word and prayer, both alone and corporately. Striking this balance in certain times and seasons in our lives in is easier said than done. The ordinary time in our lives grants us a good place to start to build routines.

Building routines begins with us. We model for our children what this looks like. I know there are different opinions on quiet time with the Lord, but I think this is a foundational building block in our spiritual lives, as well as our children's. In an ideal world this means having quiet for an extended period of time, in which we read, meditate, and pray. Life with children usually does not lend itself to such luxuries. But listen, something is better than nothing. Sometimes the only time my husband and I have to chat together uninterrupted is for about ten minutes late at night before we turn in. It is not ideal, but we relish that time. The same is true with God. Even if we only are able to spend ten minutes with him, those ten minutes are precious. If you are like me, I find that I am freshest in the morning. My best bet for getting time in with God is first thing in the morning, but this does not always happen, especially with a newborn in the house. For the most part, the kids know that when I am reading my Bible, I need a little time uninterrupted. I will admit though, this is not always the case. When I am lucky, I am able to get up before them and get some quality time in. If your kids are anything like my kids, they seem to have a sensor that goes off alerting them to the fact that I am awake, and therefore they need to be, too. Most days I simply have the make the best of it.

You may be wondering how to structure your own time with God. There is not a one size fits all when it comes to quiet time. Again, depending on your season in life, different methods will work better than others. I have done different things over the years such as in-depth Bible studies, reading and meditating on Scriptures, Scripture writing, artwork, and even more liturgical forms of daily prayer. You need to find what works best for you. The principal goal is that you are spending some time with the Lord each day.

To those nursing moms out there, take a deep breath. I know the idea of getting up early will bring you to tears. I have five kids myself. There are times that the most spiritual thing I can do for myself and my kids is sleep for an extra twenty minutes. So, the above is not geared toward you. During that season of life, I think the time you spend in the Bible with your kids is nourishing. Find podcasts to listen to while you prepare dinner, or listen to worship music in the car while driving. God understands, and he is gentle with mothers. He will guide you in what you need to be doing, and when the time is right, dig deeper into the Word again.

When our children see us taking time each day to study the Bible and pray, it shows them the value of it. We also need to spend time with our children teaching them the Bible and about God every day. Ordinary Time allows us to take the time to do that since there is not the added pressure of extra things to do such as preparing for a major holiday. Immerse yourself in God's Word and build routines and rhythms that will strengthen you and your family's walk with Jesus.

For my kids, we study the Bible throughout the day. For example, part of our school day is to do a Bible study. When the children are younger, I try to make this more activity based. Amanda White's site, *Ohamanda.com* is one of my go-to sites. She organizes resources on it such as prayer helps and movie guides and reviews. The section that I appreciate is her family devotions. She writes some one-off devotions, but also some series such as the fruit of the Spirit, and the armor of God. For each devotion she provides a Bible reading, memory verses, and ideas for easy to put together activities and crafts. Now that the two oldest are a bit older, they appreciate Kids Read Truth Bible activity books. These offer Bible passages each day as well as simple activities. Other times they color from a Bible coloring book while we talk about the Bible, or when I really have my act together, I put together different crafts and activities that I find from the internet that relate to what we are reading. If nothing else, open your Bible, read a passage, talk about it, and then pray.

If you do not homeschool, carve out time each day, or at least several times a week for concentrated Bible study and activities. I know, easier said than done. Remember, we as parents set the tone, and we ultimately decide what activities our children participate in. Maybe one day a week you choose to do a family devotion with an activity. Perhaps you decide to introduce a mealtime devotion three times a week. Our family likes *Whit's End Mealtime Devotions* for just such a thing. We read these at dinner time. They are simple and straightforward, as well as adaptable to a wide age range. Purchasing a good children's Bible and reading a story to your children at night before bed is another way to start.

We as a family spend time in prayer each night before bed. Each of us gets a turn to say a prayer and then we finish by saying the Lord's Prayer together. The baby knows that once we start praying the Lord's Prayer, bedtime is coming, and she tries to chime in. We pray for each other and any other special needs that we know of. As the kids get older, they pray for things other than just our immediate family. Now before you think this is idyllic and lovely like a Thomas Kincaid picture, you are sadly mistaken. Most nights it is a bit of a circus. We stop and start plenty of times, shush the kids who are not praying, and referee the inevitable, "He's touching me." They are kids. The practice of spending time together as a family in prayer and setting that foundational building block is vital for our kids.

RESOURCES

Resources for parents

Gross, Bobby. *Living the Christian Year: Time to Inhabit the Story of God*. Downers Grove, IL: IVP, 2009. This book is geared toward adults and offers a solid introduction to each of the major seasons of the year. He gives a fuller discussion of each season and historical background. He also offers Bible readings and reflection ideas for each week of the year. This may help parents find their own rhythm of the church year.

St. John, Heidi. *MomStrong International.* momstronginternational. com. St. John has put together a site geared toward moms, but really any woman can use it. She has two paid options for getting into God's Word. The first is a Scripture writing subscription at around $2 a month, and the second is a Bible study for about $8 per month.

She Reads Truth. shereadstruth.com. This website offers free daily online Scripture readings and devotions. They also sell hard copy Bible studies. Each day has the Scripture printed with space to write notes or prayers. The hard copy also includes study tools and other things like recipes. I find these helpful just to keep me on track. While the online version is basically the same, there is something different about the physical words in front of you and being able to mark up the pages. It also gives more room than a typical Bible would to make notes.

Resources for kids

10 Minutes of Quality Time. members.10minutesofqualitytime.com is a website that has many printables in a variety of categories. You can choose to buy a membership and have access to all the printables such as coloring sheets and crafts, or you can pay for just the group that you would like. They have a Bible activity download for $15 which gives you simple paper crafts, coloring sheets, and little books that you can print out.

Kids Read Truth. shereadstruth.com. There is a limited selection of kids' devotional books. They do have younger and older kids' books. For the younger kids, ages 6–10, the books generally have a short passage of Scripture and then an activity such as a word search or a coloring page. Each week they work on memorizing Scripture as well. For the older set, the books are geared for 11–15, and are split into boys and girls' books. There are places for notes, as well as activities.

Bowman, Crystal and Tricia Goyer. *Whit's End Mealtime Devotions: 90 Faith-Building Ideas Your Kids Will Eat Up*. Colorado Springs: Focus on the Family, 2013. This book gives you a short devotion that kids of all ages can participate in during a meal. It offers prayers, questions, and Scripture. My kids routinely ask if we can use it at dinner time. You could spend a few minutes on it or use it as a conversation starter for your meal.

Hartman, Bob. *The Play-Along Bible: Imagining God's Story through Motion and Play*. Carol Stream, IL: Tyndale Kids, 2016. This book is geared toward younger kids. Hartman condenses the Bible stories to one page and includes motions and words to say along so the kids can incorporate the stories into their bodies.

Machowski, Marty. *Long Story Short: Ten Minute Devotions to Draw Your Family to God*. Greensboro: New Growth, 2010; and *Old Story New: Ten Minute Devotions to Draw your Family to God*. Greensboro: New Growth, 2012. These two books, the former working through the Old Testament and the latter through the New, are suitable for families. He offers a five-day devotion around a Bible story or person with questions and discussion prompts. This is a good tool for parents who want a very structured time, either at dinner or if you homeschool this would also work well.

Millay, Liz. *Play Through the Bible*. Independently published, 2018. You can either download this as a pdf at https://www.steadfastfamily.com/play-through-the-bible-2/#sthash.ANrzS9Xr.dpbs or purchase a paperback copy through Amazon. This is a resource for younger kids. For each of the fifteen Old Testament Bible stories she provides a teaching, activities, snacks, and crafts. They are easy to do, many with things you have around the house already. She overlaps with some of what I propose for Lent, so if you wanted different activities, or simply want to go through the major OT stories, I recommend this book.

White, Amanda. *OhAmanda.com*. She offers devotions with different activities for kids, as well as resources for parents. If you are looking for a fun way to integrate the Bible and activities into your life, you need to check this site.

Bibles

Hastings, Selina. *DK Illustrated Children's Bible*. New York: DK Children, 2004. Unlike other children's Bibles, DK's includes a greater number of stories, even the harder ones such as Jephthah's daughter. As with all DK books, it has pictures, facts, and tidbits to give a fuller picture of the story. Your children can grow into this Bible and use it as a resource. There are several editions, so simply find one.

Lloyd–Jones, Sally. *The Jesus Storybook Bible: Every Story Whispers His Name*. Nashville: Zonderkidz, 2006. This is probably my favorite children's Bible. It is not comprehensive, in that as with most children's Bibles it does not have every story, but it does have many of them. In each story Lloyd-Jones shows how the Old Testament points to Jesus, as well as how we learn more about Jesus in the New Testament. It is wonderfully written and beautifully illustrated. I highly recommend it for young kids.

Lloyd–Jones, Sally. *The Jesus Storybook Bible Coloring Book*. Nashville: Zonderkidz, 2020. This book follows along with the *Jesus Storybook Bible* and offers children wonderful pages to color. If your child is a kinesthetic learner, consider purchasing a copy so he can color while you read.

Tales that Tell the Truth. Charlotte: The Good Book Company. This is a series of illustrated Bible stories that dig a little deeper and not only tell the story, but also get into the theological truth it teaches. They are wonderfully illustrated, and I recommend any of them.

Young, Sarah. *Jesus Calling Storybook*. Nashville: Thomas Nelson, 2012. Young shows how the entire Bible, indeed all of God's creation points to Jesus. The number of stories included is limited, but it gives a good starting point for children to understand how all of creation, and all the stories in the Bible point to Jesus.

5

Fat Tuesday, Ash Wednesday, and Lent

HISTORY AND THEOLOGY

The longest penitential season in the church's calendar is Lent. While Advent takes place in the midst of Christmas preparations and the natural inclination to enjoy the oncoming winter, Lent takes place in the doldrums of the year. The church historically prepared people for baptism during this time. It also leads up to the holiest days of the year—Jesus's death and resurrection. These are the days that changed everything. As such, the time of preparation before the feast is more intense, and generally includes fasting.

Lent is the forty-day period before Easter. Since Sundays are never fasting days because they always celebrate the resurrection of our Lord, Lent begins on Ash Wednesday to add the necessary extra days. The whole season lasts forty-six days. Historically, people fasted on Mondays, Wednesdays, and Fridays. For some this was a complete fast of not eating, for many others this meant to fast from meat, or in some cases even animal products such as milk and cheese. In the Orthodox Church they fast from all animal products for the duration of Lent. In other words, this is a strict fast, and it can be a hardship.

The length of Lent comes from the example that Jesus gave us during his time in the wilderness. He spent forty days and forty nights fasting and praying, and then Satan tempted him. It also reminds us of the forty years the Israelites wandered in the desert, and the forty days that the rain came down during the great flood. It is interesting to note that the Hebrew word for wilderness, *midbar*, has as its root the word *debar*, which means word or thing. Walking in the desert does not mean that God is absent. In fact, it is often in the middle of the desert that we meet with God—we come face to face with his Word. Without the distractions of daily life, we see more clearly what God is doing. We are also more desperate for him to act. The idea of fasting for the forty days allows us to make an annual journey into the desert in order to strip away everything except for him. We realize once again our utter dependence upon God.

In the early church Lent prepared people for baptism. During the time in which the Roman Empire declared Christianity illegal, the church closely guarded itself by limiting baptism. Catechumens, people learning and preparing to be members of the church, spent three years in study and training before becoming full members. Catechumens devoted a significant amount of time learning the doctrines and teachings of the church before gaining admittance into the full life of the church. They needed to understand what they were signing on to. So instead of participating in Communion during the worship service, lest they intended to report to non-Christians spurious accounts of Christian practices, they engaged in further study and learning. Therefore, baptism acted as an initiation into the full life of the church, which included Holy Communion.

The season starts with Ash Wednesday, however, many people who follow Lent also celebrate Fat Tuesday or Shrove Tuesday. Shrove comes from the word shrive, which means to confess your sins. Before embarking on the upcoming season of fasting and penance, people first finished the last of their winter stores. As such, Lent conveniently occurs in the agricultural year. This is why many cultures have some sort of pancake or donut that is traditional to eat on Fat Tuesday. Many churches today provide a pancake supper.

Ash Wednesday is a day of fasting and penance. Many people fast, or fast meat products, or only eat one small meal that day. Most churches which celebrate Ash Wednesday offer a worship service on that day and impose ashes on people's foreheads. The ashes come from the previous year's blessed palms left over from Palm Sunday. As the congregants receive the ashes, the minister usually says something along the lines of: "Remember you are from dust and to dust you shall return." It reminds us of our own mortality as well the effects of sin in our lives, and how it causes our lives to become dust.

For many Christians today Lent represents a time to make changes in their lives. Fasting remains a cornerstone for the season even for people not preparing for baptism. Corporately, the body of Christ recognizes our dependence on Jesus, who is our true Bread of Life. Popular fasts include fasting from meat on Fridays (hence McDonald's increased advertising of Fillet-O-Fish during Lent), or fasting a meal week, or fasting for a day a week, fasting from desserts, or fasting from social media. By giving up these things you gain more time to spend with God. Some people concentrate on adding a discipline to their lives, such as Bible reading, quiet time, or some other type of devotion.

HOW CAN I GET STARTED?

Lent is a really special time for our family. My kids actually look forward to it because of the activities we do during this time. As part of the rhythm that we have established for our family since the kids were very small, they simply expect it to happen. Our kids do not fast yet, because they are still young. They do ask questions about it because they see me model it for them.

I take fasting seriously. For many years I have given up desserts during Lent. I remember fasting from desserts as young as middle school. For me, it represents taking the sweetness of life away because without God, without Jesus's sacrifice, life loses its sweetness. It presents me with a tangible reminder of the beauty of who God is. It also makes me conscious of what I am eating, and

I won't lie, I look forward to Easter more when I fast from sweets than when I do not. Living with discipline is hard, but worth it.

I also attempt to fast from meat on Fridays. I have been more and less successful with this during the years. Living with a husband who is a self-proclaimed meatatrian, and who grew up Pentecostal with no notion of Lent has been a learning curve for both of us. He, again because of his background, does not observe Lent. He does not feel that he needs it to celebrate Easter. I do. Since I plan our meals, I try to fix meatless meals on Fridays. I find that while I can easily plan a meatless meal for dinner, lunch sometimes slips through the cracks if we have leftovers, or sometimes we have lunch with Brian at the school where he teaches. Modeling food choices during Lent creates an indelible impression on children. My Catholic aunts and uncles still remember having to fast from meat on Fridays, and the types of meals they would eat. Etched into their memory, they still recall some of their favorite, and not so favorite meatless meals.

If your kids are old enough to participate in some sort of fast, your family may decide what you want to do with the money you saved from fasting. Your kids may want to give it to a local charity such as a food bank, or the church, or even to a special cause. They will see how being disciplined and obedient affects not only their family, but also a wider audience. Your obedience as a family helps another family in need.

Another fast I have found helpful is to fast from TV. Rarely do I say, well, that was time well spent watching that show. I find that I have more time to do other things such as read. Sometimes I choose a Christian living book, or a history of Christianity book to read during Lent. Since this type of fast is not potentially detrimental to a child's growth, I see limiting technology as a useful fast for kids. By limiting the time using technology such TV or tablets, you open up time for your children to engage in the Word. If you are struggling to find time to get into the Word as a family, this may be a good place to start. View this time of Lent as an opportunity to strengthen your walk with the Lord, not simply to engage in a diet plan or self-betterment. It truly is a precious time.

Beyond fasting, you may ask what can I do? The plethora of Advent activities overshadows the relative dearth of Lent activities for children. Searching for Lent activities for kids usually yields a list of forty things to do, which have little progression or coherence. To fill in the gap, I devised a six-week basic curriculum for my kids that I share below. I use it as a guide each year to give shape to our time together as we walk through the wilderness of Lent.

RESOURCES

Drew, Ed. *The Wonder of Easter: An Easter journey for the whole family*. Charlotte: The Good Book Company, 2019. This book walks through family devotions for the season of Lent. It gives some activity ideas and questions for different age groups, so that all family members can participate. We use this at dinner time.

Foster, Richard. *Celebration of Discipline: The Path to Spiritual Growth Special 20th Anniversary Edition*. New York: Harper Collins, 2000. Foster's classic about the spiritual disciplines is a must have for all Christians. He outlines twelve disciplines and how people can incorporate them into their lives. This is an excellent tool to have in your spiritual toolbox. You may choose to work on one of the disciplines during Lent.

Love, Vernie Schorr. *Spiritual Disciplines for Children: A Guide to a Deeper Spiritual Life for You and Your Children*. Lafayette, CO: Character Choice, 2012. Love uses Foster's *Celebration of Discipline* as her guide to develop practices and disciplines for children. She gives practical ways for parents to instill the spiritual disciplines in their children. Again, you may choose to work on one or two disciplines during Lent with your kids.

LENTEN ACTIVITIES FOR YOUR FAMILY

When I think about Lent, I think about the silence God's people endured for 400 years between the time of the prophets and Jesus. I think about the reality of the world before Jesus came, and how people must have felt while walking in darkness. I also think about the fact that God always has a plan and is faithful to his promises. With these thoughts in mind, I devised a pattern for my kids to follow for the six weeks in Lent. We focus on the covenants, basically salvation history, and this culminates with Easter. While no two years look exactly alike, I do hit the main points each year. What follows is a guide for how you may want to approach Lent.

I concentrate on the covenants that God made with his people because these form the foundation for our relationship with him. Further, Jesus' life, death, and resurrection only makes sense in the context of the previous covenants. Today we may think of a covenant as a contract or simply an agreement, but a covenant entails so much more than that. A contract becomes null and void rather easily. A covenant binds two parties together, is based on promises, and therefore is harder to break. Marriages are covenants because they are more than simply contracts, they bring two people together to be one in a new way based on promises. In the same sense, the covenants that God made with his people represent so much more than simply contracts. God promises his people that he will be their God, and he will uphold his end of the covenant no matter what. Even when we break that covenant, God continues to keep his end of the deal. Jesus' death on the cross fulfills the covenants, and his resurrection institutes the new covenant.

A note. We read a portion of the story every day, or we reread the story. I find tactile learners enjoy listening better if they have something to do. This past year I found coloring sheets online for what we were talking about that day, or they colored a page from a coloring book such as *The Jesus Storybook Coloring Book*. Sometimes this completes our activity for the day if that is what everyone is up to. That is ok. Below I suggest different crafts and activities you can do with your kids, but you know your kids best. Don't feel bound to these. Sometimes these work well with my family, and other years they want no part of something they loved the previous year. Sometimes we do every single activity, and other years we only hit a few. These ideas are meant to help you to think about how to incorporate Lent into your lives. If you can't do something every day, that is ok, too.

Ash Wednesday

Lent begins on Ash Wednesday. Sometimes for us, we observe Ash Wednesday as a quiet day. Sometimes, that is not possible. Instead of using ashes to remind yourselves that we are from dust and to dust we shall return, you can take a black marker and mark a cross on your kids' hands. Remind them that we were made from the earth, and to the earth we will return. Although admittedly a bit morbid, kids understand that we do not live forever. I emphasize that we were made to be in relationship with God, and Jesus, by his life, death, and resurrection makes this possible. It is a day to remember that we are sinful, yet through this upcoming journey of Lent, we see that God does not leave us in our sinfulness.

The days following Ash Wednesday spend some time on contrition, and how we adopt an attitude of humility. Teach your children how to confess to God and to each other. We model how to say prayers to God asking for forgiveness. We as parents also demonstrate this with our kids in that we are quick to ask for forgiveness from them when we do something wrong, and work to change our behavior.

Suggested Scripture: Psalm 103.

Suggested Scripture for Thursday: Jonah 3.

Stress that once the Ninevites knew what they did wrong, they sought to change their ways. Come up with action plans with your children on how they can make better choices.

Suggested Scripture for Friday: Psalm 51.

This Psalm offers a good vocabulary about how we understand God's forgiveness and our sin. By using this Psalm early in life, it will be easier for our children to understand the depth of their sin later in life. Remind them that whenever we sin, we are really sinning against God, and we cannot make it better. We need Jesus to save us.

Week 1: God's Creation, Genesis 1:1–2:4

This week we study God's good creation. When God created the earth and the universe, he called it good. Sometimes we downplay the goodness of creation because we see so much that is broken, but this earth is the home that God intended for us. The earth around us also bears the scars of sin, but God called the original creation good. The earth is our home and we humans, as the pinnacle of creation, exercise dominion in the world because God created us in his image. We can get caught up with all the bad things around us, but the original creation made with joy and goodness, reflects our good God and creator.

God issues the first covenant in Genesis 1. He creates humans in his image. The new people, called to be fruitful and multiply, have dominion over the earth. God demonstrates the uniqueness of himself and also humans: we have a relationship with him and others.

Suggested Memory Verse: Genesis 1:31

Suggested Activities

On the first day we focus on light. Go under a blanket and use a flashlight to create light and retell the story.

On day two we draw attention to vegetation. Try planting some seeds in a small planter and watching them grow throughout the rest of Lent. If you want, decorate the planter, such as a paper cup or a small clay pot. Plants like grass will grow quickly.

On day three we highlight the sun, stars, and moon. We make a mobile of them. You may choose to make a sun out of construction paper or a paper plate. It changes each year for us. Do you want to experiment with clouds? Try this: cut a small portion of Ivory soap (it has to be Ivory) and put it in the microwave to 30–40 seconds. This creates a cloud!

On day four we concentrate on the animals God made. Let your child choose her favorite animal and make it out of air-drying clay. When dry, color or paint it.

On day five we emphasize the creation of humans. Trace your child either on a large piece of paper, or if it is nice outside on the sidewalk with chalk. Decorate it and write, God made me!

Extras

Zager, Ellen Kahan and Harriet Helfand. *And there was Evening and there was Morning*. Minneapolis: Kar–Ben, 2018. This is a stunning book that uses rhyme to tell the story of creation. All the pictures are made out of the corresponding Hebrew words. I highly recommend this book.

Ray, Jane. *The Story of Creation: Words from Genesis*. Boston: Dutton Books, 1993. Ray's bright illustrations are detailed, lovely, and depict many aspects of the Garden of Eden. She uses the Bible as her text. The pictures are gorgeous, and so it gives your children something to look at while reading the Bible.

Week 2: The Fall, Sin, and the Flood, Genesis 3; 6—9

Every year is a bit different. Sometimes I do get into the Fall in the first week, but most times, I leave it to the second week. We talk about how pain and suffering entered the world. Kids start to understand that it is through our disobedience that sin entered, and continues to enter, into the world. I usually only spend one day on the Fall.

Noah offers a contrast of obedience to Adam and Eve's disobedience. God caused the flood due to humanity's sin. People forgot their first covenant with God and did their own things. At the end of the flood narrative God institutes a new covenant. God places a rainbow in the sky. When you read the Hebrew, it is pictured as a military bow. In the ancient Near East this iconography was prevalent. When a god went off to war, the bow faced up. When the army returned victoriously, the bow hung down, showing the god at peace. Here we have a reminder in nature that God wars no longer with his creation. He renews his covenant with Noah and calls him to obedience. We focus on the fact that even when people disobey, God makes a way for us to remain in relationship with him.

Suggested Memory Verse: Genesis 9:13

Suggested Activities

On day one we focus on the consequences of sin. Following directions can be hard. Playing a simple game of Simon Says is a fun way to think about obedience.

On day two we look at Noah's obedience in building the ark. Find a picture of the ark to color or try to build an ark out of things like Legos or blocks.

On day three we gather all the animals into the ark. Build a small ark out of a box or a basket in your home and gather your stuffed animals into it. Imagine what it must have been like to get all those animals in, housed, and fed!

On day four we talk about how the ark floated for so long. A fun activity is to construct boats and see if they will float. Use whatever you have around the house: tin foil, Legos, milk containers, your choice. Then, if you are really ambitious, add animals or figures to your boat to see if it still floats.

On day five we concentrate on the rainbow, and God's covenant with Noah and all humanity. We make salt dough rainbows. Mix ½ cup of salt with 1 cup of flour, and moisten with water, about 3/8 cup, until a workable dough forms. Then your kids can enjoy playing with it for a little bit before shaping their rainbow. To set it you need to bake it. We usually use the speedy way, which is to zap it in the microwave for about 30 to 60 seconds at a time until it is hard. Now your rainbows are ready to be painted.

Extras

Pinkney, Jerry. *Noah's Ark*. San Francisco: Chronicle Books, 2002. Pickney won a Caldecott Honor for this book. His pictures are realistic, yet gentle at the same time.

Spier, Peter. *Noah's Ark*. New York: Double Day Books for Young Readers, 1977. This is a wordless picture book, and each picture has lots of things to see. Spier has a bit of sense of humor, and some of the pictures have things that both kids and adults will enjoy.

Week 3: Abraham, Genesis 12:1–9; 15; 18; 21–22

The third week we usually spend talking about Abraham. God shows his faithfulness through Abraham. Jesus fulfills the covenant God made with Abraham with his death on the cross and resurrection. In Genesis 15 God institutes the Abrahamic covenant, and it happens years before Isaac is born. The flaming cook pot going between the broken animals depicts God walking the covenant. You see, back in the time of Abraham people would cut a covenant. They would cut animals and walk through them saying that if they would break this covenant, then what has happened to these animals should happen to them. That is pretty stern stuff. But if you notice, Abraham does not walk through the animals, only God does. In essence God declares that if either party breaks the covenant, God will take the penalty on himself. It will be God's body that is broken in two. And what happened on the cross? That very thing. Jesus' body was broken in two, his blood shed to fulfill the covenant that God made with Abraham.

For young kids, this is a bit over their heads. The birth of Isaac takes most of our attention. God's faithfulness to give Abraham a son, even when both Abraham and Sarah are really old, exhibits God's character. We know we can trust him.

Suggested Memory Verse: Genesis 22:17

Suggested Activities

On the first day, we learn about the journey that Abraham made from Ur to Canaan. This was a very long trip, even stopping in Haran. I show my kids a map of his journey, and if they are old enough (at least six), have them draw their own map of his journey. My kids also make forts to represent how Abraham lived in tents and traveled.

On day two, we remember the promises God made to Abraham. He promised that Abraham's descendants would be like the stars. Find a coloring sheet online with stars on it. Make spirals out of construction paper and attached stars to them. When they get older, I will talk about the actual covenant that God made with Abraham in Genesis 15. You could have your children place stuffed animals out, and then walk through them to symbolize what ancient covenants meant.

On day three we learn about Abraham's family. We talk about how God keeps his promises. Draw a large tree on paper and then put your handprints on it to show that you are part of Abraham's family tree as well. We also sing Father Abraham, which is one of my favorite kids songs.

On day four we discuss the binding of Isaac. This is a hard lesson for kids, so you need to choose things that are age appropriate. It can be a little scary for kids, but at the same time, I think they concentrate more on the sheep in a thicket, than a father offering his son as a sacrifice. God will provide even when we are unsure how this will happen. We color a picture of Abraham and Isaac, but you could also make a sheep, and cover it with cotton balls.

On day five we talk about Abraham interceding for Sodom and Gomorrah, which is actually before the birth of Isaac. I emphasize that Abraham had a relationship with God that allowed him to intercede for the people. We make soft pretzels. The shape of the pretzel is said to represent praying hands. As a righteous man, Abraham represents a man who prays. Soft pretzels are pretty fun to make, too.

Extras

Bader, Joanne. *Abraham, Sarah, and Isaac: (Arch Book)*. St. Louis: Concordia, 2011. The Arch Books series is a delightful one. There are so many, and they cover much of the Bible. This one has bright pictures and of course a rhyming story about God's faithfulness to Abraham and Sarah.

Washburn, Donna Washburn and Heather Butt. *300 Best Bread Machine Recipes*. Toronto: Robert Rose, 2012. This is a fantastic bread machine book, and they have a good soft pretzel recipe. Just remember to boil the pretzels in water with about 2 tablespoons to ¼ c baking soda for about 30 seconds per side for that pretzel taste and shine.

Week 4: Jacob and Joseph, Genesis 24; 25:19–24; 27–29; 32:22–31; 37; 41–46

To set the stage of what will happen in Egypt, I usually spend time talking about Jacob and Joseph. Children need to understand how the Israelites got into Egypt. Of course, the story of Joseph is a powerful one, and if you choose, you could easily spend a few days on it, talking about the hardships that Joseph faced, and how he must have felt forgotten by God. When your little one feels out of place, the story of Joseph reminds him that God is still working. God is ultimately in control, even when things are not going our way.

Suggested Memory Verse: Genesis 28:15

Suggested Activities

On day one, we learn about the marriage of Isaac and Rebekah. I like to point out that Rebekah had a lot of faith to leave her home and marry someone she had never met. We make jewelry for this day. This can be really simple, such as making beaded bracelets or necklaces, since Abraham's servant gave Rebekah jewelry and money.

On day two, we talk about the birth of Jacob and Esau, and how they had a sibling rivalry from the beginning. We also talk about how each of the parents had their favorite, and why this is going to cause problems when Jacob and Esau grow up. One year we made bean bag dolls. My original idea was to make one smooth and the other one hairy, but to be honest, this simply didn't happen. My three oldest kids worked on them. They were just sort of put together. I drew a kind of gingerbread man shape on the fabric, cut, and sewed. They came out looking a little odd, not to mention the fact that one of my kids decided to use plaid for his fabric. As with most of the crafts we do, it is more about doing it than creating the perfect craft. This was actually something they really enjoyed doing.

On day three we see how Jacob gained Esau's birthright and blessing, and then how he ran away. We talk about his vision of the angels descending and ascending on a ladder. Make a ladder of some sort. This past year, my kids made a tower out of toilet paper and paper towels, but you can also draw a ladder, or use popsicle sticks and glue to make a small ladder.

On day four, we concentrate on Jacob's sons and daughter. Now, it is a little hard to explain all the wives and the handmaidens. I don't spend too much time on that. I draw attention to Joseph's brothers' jealousy toward him because he was Jacob's favorite. We talk about his dreams and his multi-colored coat, and how this drives Joseph's brothers to throw him in a pit, and he ends up being sold as a slave. We take either coffee filters or paper towels and draw random designs with markers. Then we spray the filters with water and watch the marker color bleed and make a pretty design. All of my kids are able to do this craft. Then, if you want, you can cut them to look like a coat, or use them for decoration.

On day five we think about how Joseph ended up in Egypt and what God did through him. God used Joseph where he was, even though he went through great hardships, to save not only Egypt, but also his own family. Play a game with M&Ms or beans to show how God provided for Egypt. Give your kids a certain amount of M&Ms, or any small candy. They will get the same amount for each "year." So, let's say you give them ten each. Then, you collect two from each of them, and save them. They have to eat one, sell four, and use three to plant for the next season. Then they get ten more, for seven years. Once the famine starts, decrease the number of candies each person gets to illustrate how they needed to rely on Joseph's system of saving the food.

Extras

Koralek, Jenny. *The Coat of Many Colors*. Grand Rapids: Eerdmans Books for Young Readers, 2004. This very stylized book tells the Joseph story. It is a good resource to use since it is more detailed than most story book Bibles, but not as long as the Biblical text.

LaDuca, Rob and Robert Ramirez, dirs. *Joseph: King of Dreams*. Glendale, CA: DreamWorks, 2000. While this is a Hollywood movie, and they do take some liberties, it is still a nice wholesome movie to watch. My kids enjoyed watching it, and you can always talk about the discrepancies between the biblical text and the movie.

Week 5: The Exodus, Exodus: 1–13, 20

The Exodus is the bedrock of Jewish faith, and it provides the template for our understanding of Christ's work on the cross. It lays the groundwork for Passover, and we cannot understand Jesus' sacrifice without understanding Passover. The plagues are easy to talk about, and we spend a day only talking about them. I make sure I devote at least one day talking about Passover. We discuss the angel of death and how it passed over the children of Israel. I then relate this to how when we believe in Jesus, his blood acts the same way. The angel of death passes over us as well, and we have eternal life with God. I really don't think that you can state that too many times, so even if you talked about the Passover recently, it won't hurt to do it again.

If you are very ambitious, you can also include the giving of the Law, which is the actual Mosaic covenant. Here God outlines very clearly what is expected from the Israelites in the giving of the Ten Commandments, and in return how he will be their God. The Israelites accept God's terms of the covenant, both blessings and curses. I have struggled with bringing this part of the story to life with my kids. I tried having my kids make tablets out of cardboard, but they were less than interested. For older kids imparting the rules and expectations of the law, along with the blessings and curses the Israelites agreed to, illustrates how living a godly life benefits you. If you run out of time this week, Monday of next week easily works as well.

Suggested Memory Verse: Exodus 12:13
(You can focus on the first part for younger kids.)

Suggested Activities

On the first day we talk about how God protected Moses as a young baby. We read the story of his mother placing him in the Nile, and how Pharaoh's daughter adopted him. I emphasize that God had a plan and protected Moses through everything. We color sheets about Moses, and then we make a basket out of paper.

On the second day we look at how Moses ran away from Egypt after killing an Egyptian and ended up in Midian where he met and married Zipporah. We then focus on his call through the burning bush. We draw and color a picture of the burning bush and add red and orange tissue paper to make it look like it is burning.

On the third day we discuss the first nine plagues. God hardened Pharaoh's heart and used this hardness to show his power over Pharaoh and the false gods of Egypt. We imagine what the different plagues must have been like. Draw pictures of the different plagues. Below I have a link to a site on how to make an origami frog as a representation of one of the plagues.

On the fourth day we detail the tenth plague and the Passover. We make matzah. The institution of Passover also included the institution of the Feast of Unleavened Bread since the Israelites were called to make bread without yeast. Now for matzah to be kosher, it has to be completed within 18 minutes. Guess what, ours never is finished that quickly, so it is never kosher, but the kids love to make it. Flour usually covers the table, our matzah is nowhere near as thin as it should be, and I always feel like I need to cook it a little longer because it doesn't look done in the four minutes it is supposed to be. It is still yummy, and my kids always ask to make it.

On the fifth day we act out the crossing of the Red Sea. Very simply, the kids take turns being Moses, Pharaoh, the Children of Israel, and the soldiers. Each reenactment takes about two minutes, and we usually do it more than once. We also watch the *Prince of Egypt*. While there are some historical inaccuracies, for the most part it stays true to the story. I don't let them watch it during other parts of the year, so it is a special treat.

Extras

Batyah. "Matzah." *All Recipes*. https://www.allrecipes.com/recipe/213682/matzah/. This is a very easy and straightforward recipe for matzah.

Chapman, Brenda and Steve Hickner, dirs. *The Prince of Egypt*. Glendale, CA: DreamWorks, 1998. Again, while this movie does take some artistic license, it is still wonderfully done. The songs are catchy, and it focuses on the struggle Moses must have felt going back to Egypt and seeing people he would have known.

Guenther, Leanne. "Weave a Basket Paper Craft." *DLTK's Site for Kids Growing Together.* http://www.dltk-bible.com/crafts/mbasketweave.htm. Here is a simple basket weaving craft.

Peter. "How to Fold an Easy Origami Jumping Frog." *Origami.me.* https://origami.me/jumping-frog/. This is an easy how-to for folding a jumping frog. I suggest using the thinnest paper you have.

Holy Week

This leads us to Holy Week. As you finish your Lenten journey this week you walk with Jesus in his last days. If your church makes a big deal of it, then I personally wouldn't see the need to go over the top throughout the week. You may want to do some extra activities on Monday and Tuesday, but if you have the opportunity for corporate Wednesday, Thursday, Friday, and Saturday worship, the following may not really apply to you. For those who are not familiar with what happens on these days, typically you have a Tenebrae service on Wednesday, which consists of readings and Psalms and the extinguishing of candles. Thursday is Maundy Thursday and may include a foot washing and the stripping of the altar, followed by the watch. Friday, of course, has Good Friday services. Saturday can have two different services. There may be an early Saturday service, but from what I have known, this is not very popular. The highest feast day of the year is the Easter Vigil on Saturday night.

The week starts with Palm Sunday. I think most churches have some sort of Palm Sunday celebration, even if it is only handing out palms and reading the corresponding Scripture passage. We celebrate Jesus' triumphal entry into Jerusalem. People hailed him as the Messiah—the Anointed One. They saw him as the one who would break the oppression of Rome. Since we join in corporate worship for this day, I do not plan other activities.

For the rest of Holy Week, I plan a daily activity using Amanda White's *Sense of the Resurrection* as a guide. She outlines simple ideas rooted in Scripture. I pick one or two activities for the children to complete for each day. On Wednesday, Thursday, and Friday I also try to cook simple or vegetarian meals as a way to simplify our lives and focus on Jesus' suffering.

On Wednesday, we typically celebrate by participating in a shortened Tenebrae service with my kids. The Tenebrae service consists of the reading of Psalms and Bible passages and the gradual extinguishing of candles. It is a service that takes place at night, so by the time it is finished, the church is quite dark, and the people leave in darkness. We contemplate, lament (many of the readings come from Lamentations), and prepare ourselves for Good Friday.

For our Tenebrae service, we light candles after lunch because we usually have church at night. Our church does not deviate from its regularly scheduled programs on this Wednesday, so the afternoon is a time for us to be quiet together as a family. While the typical Tenebrae service lasts about an hour or so, we shorten it considerably to about fifteen minutes at the most. We read three readings and three Psalms. We then extinguish candles, one after each reading. To be honest, the kids care more about blowing out the candles than listening, but my hope and prayer is that through the years this will become an important part of their Holy Week journey.

Thursday is Maundy Thursday. The name comes from the Latin, *mandatum*, or commandment. Jesus gave a new commandment, and so this day commemorates the institution of Communion. It is a day of both joy and sorrow. We rejoice that we have Communion as a way to remember Jesus. But we also sorrow because we know that this is the night on which Jesus was betrayed. It is bittersweet. In many liturgical churches this will be a night that has many parts. Pastors wash their parishioners' feet, and all join in Holy Communion. Then comes a portion of the service that I find to be one of the most poignant in all the year—the stripping of the altar. As the congregation recites Psalm 22, a small group of people take everything off of the front. All the decorations, all the candles, everything comes off except for the altar itself. Then someone will wash the altar. I still remember how a church I attended while I was in college approached washing the altar. Three women dressed in black cassocks slowly, so slowly and meticulously, washed the altar in complete silence. I still cry when I think of it. The pain that Jesus underwent simmers beneath the surface. The congregation leaves in silence and darkness after this. Some churches will then have a watch; this is a continual prayer time from the end of the service until the morning. Some churches leave a room open for this, or have people pray in their homes.

Our church that we attend now does not celebrate Maundy Thursday. Since I grew up with Maundy Thursday being a large part of my Holy Week experience, I do make a strong effort to instill the sense of expectation and sorrow for my kids. We like to make matzah again. For a couple of years I tried to serve a nice meal on Thursday to represent the meal that Jesus might have had with his disciples, but I have come to the conclusion that this takes away from the Easter celebration, so I have reverted back to simple meals, such as sandwiches with soup. We talk about the Last Supper, and what it meant to the disciples who had a Jewish understanding, and further how it points to Jesus. I wash my kids' feet and talk about Jesus as I do it. As my kids get older, we may have extended prayer times after dinner.

Good Friday is one of the most significant days of the year. It is somber and hard to get through because we recognize the suffering that Jesus went through for our sake, not his own. When we sit down and think about it, it is heartbreaking that our God had to go to such lengths for us. For me, this is not a day to be playing loud music. While there is celebration in it, I think our primary response is to be quiet and mournful on this day. Good Friday gives us one last look at the gravity of our sin and the reality of the sacrifice. We should be on our knees repenting and recognizing the awesome justice of God. If your church offers a service that is somber, I would highly recommend it. Depending on the ages of your children, this may or may not be appropriate for them. Some churches do offer childcare or children's services during the Good Friday service, and I would say take advantage of these. Even if your kids are not able to participate in the service, they will get into the rhythm of going to church on Good Friday.

This is a day to remember our sin. We count the cost of what Christ did for us. This is not a day to throw a party. Today we all sit at the foot of the cross and contemplate Jesus' death. We need to see the pain that this caused our Father and our Brother. We cannot skip from the glory of Palm Sunday and Jesus's triumphant entry into Jerusalem to Jesus's triumph over death without first wrestling with the death itself. This is a funeral day, and as such we should be quiet and remorseful.

At home, I try to make it a quiet day. I recognize that being silent and still is impossible for most kids, but they can be for a few minutes. They can also redirect their energy. One of my friends remembers Good Fridays growing up, and she said that her family would spend the morning cleaning. I have always thought what a good way to spend part of the day. Devote the morning, or a few hours in the afternoon having everyone tackle a task. While cleaning, ponder on the atonement, and how Christ washes us from the inside out. While cleaning may not appear spiritual, it can be. It places us in a humble position to recognize the amazing work Jesus did. It also readies our house for the upcoming Easter celebration.

From my time in Canada, I picked up the tradition of eating hot cross buns on Good Friday. If you are not familiar, they are small buns that are usually spiced with cinnamon and can have raisins or currants in them. The top is cut to look like a cross, and if you use icing, you put it in a cross shape as well. For us, we make the basic cinnamon hot cross bun, cut the cross, and that is it. I recommend Washburn and Butt's book of bread machine recipes for their hot cross buns recipe.

For activities, I recommend utilizing Amanda White's *Sense of the Resurrection*. I select three or four activities for the kids to do throughout the day. It breaks up the day, and reminds the kids that Jesus endured the cross for hours. It keeps Jesus front and center throughout the day.

My favorite church service of the year is the Easter Vigil. At the church where I grew up, it was an amazing event. The Vigil rehearses salvation history. It starts in the darkness of Lent. We light a candle outside the church and bring it in saying, "The light of Christ." After this we read different stories from the Old Testament. The church where I grew up assigned different readings to each Sunday School class, and each class would then prepare a skit depicting the story.

Then part way through the service, we switch from Lent to Easter. The lights come on, we ring bells, and sing "Jesus Christ is Risen Today, Alleluia!" All the decorations and everything that had been stripped from the altar on Maundy Thursday returns.

I say all of this to say this, most churches do not observe the Easter Vigil. So, why not create a Vigil tradition in your home? I have to be honest, this one has been a bit of a hard sell to my kiddos. This past year it actually worked, with my oldest being eight. We looked at the different options to act out, and each child chose one or two. The Red Sea Crossing is required, and they like to do that one because the Egyptians die in the water. We also acted out Noah. Two of my kids decided to be animals, and we all crowded on a bed as an ark. My son's favorite story is Jesus calming the storm, so even though it is not one of the Old Testament texts, or even one of the New Testament texts, we acted it out as well. All of the kids got into the action, and I think they understood the stories a bit better. You can also simply read these stories and talk about the history of how God saved his people in the past, and how he will continue to do so in the future. After remembering God's saving power to Israel, transition into Easter. Ring bells, sing, clap, dance. Read the story of the empty tomb and rejoice in the gift of salvation.

Extras

Suggested readings for an Easter Vigil: Gen 1:1–2a; Gen 7:1–5, 11–18, 8:6–18, 9:8–13; Gen 22:1–18; Ex 14:10–31, 15:20–21; Isaiah 55:1–11; Ezk 36:24–28; Ezk 37:1–4; Zep 3:14–20; Rom 6:3–11; Luke 24:1–12.

White, Amanda. *A Sense of the Resurrection: An Easter Experience for Families.* Amanda White, 2014. This can be found at http://ohamanda.com/a-sense-of-the-resurrection-an-easter-experience-for-families/. She offers a twelve-day guide for Scripture readings and activities. I find that it is more helpful for what I do to combine some activities on days and leave out others that simply do not work.

6

Easter and the Easter Season

HISTORY AND THEOLOGY

Also known as Resurrection Sunday, this is the day that we celebrate the resurrection of Jesus—the day that everything changed. No longer a simple martyr for his cause, Jesus' resurrection heralds him as the king of all things, triumphant even over death. While we do not know all the ins and outs of exactly how Jesus accomplished our salvation, we do know that the empty tomb on Sunday morning announced Jesus' victory. Our sins have been nailed to the cross, and we can now rise with Christ. Alleluia!

Since Christ's resurrection happened on a Sunday, it became the new primary day of worship for most Christians, many of whom had been Jews and worshipped on Saturdays. The move from Saturday to Sunday seems to have happened relatively early in the history of Christianity. By the first century of the church, most Christians met together on Sundays. All Sundays became little Easters to remind followers that Jesus rose on the first day of the week, and that if we believe in him, we will rise, too.

The date of Easter changes every year since it is tied to the lunar cycle and the vernal equinox. Namely it is the Sunday after the first full moon after the vernal equinox. It may or may not line up with Passover, the Jewish feast during which Jesus was crucified.

Our Orthodox brothers and sisters celebrate Easter based upon the Julian instead of Gregorian calendar, so theirs is often later than most Western churches'. The debate over the date of Easter has caused much consternation in the church throughout the centuries. Easter only makes sense with the backdrop of Passover. Passover celebrates the Israelites' freedom from Egypt through God's final plague—the death of the firstborn. God tells the Israelites to sacrifice a lamb and spread its blood over their door. When they do this, the angel of death will pass over their house and not take their firstborn; they are covered with sacrificial blood. Jesus becomes our sacrificial lamb, with the angel of death passing over us as well so that we may enjoy eternal life with God. This is the new covenant made with the shed blood of Jesus.

On a liturgical note, the season of Easter lasts fifty days until the day of Pentecost. Easter changes everything, and we need to live into this new reality every day. We are called to be resurrection people all the time. Entering into that lifestyle can be hard, and requires discipline and practice, which the Easter season promotes. The old saying goes, it takes twenty-one days to make a habit, and only three days to break it. This time allows us to get into the Easter season.

HOW CAN I GET STARTED?

Most churches have some sort of Easter celebration, whether it is just during the normal worship times, or sometimes they add extras such as a sunrise service. I am sure that your church home has traditions in place and so do you. I would imagine that these are important to you, and I would not wish to change them. If, however you do not have traditions for this day, you may think about trying some.

If you are like most people, Easter morning is spent in church. After spending the season of Lent preparing, now we enter into the Easter celebration full of joy. I find that I am more excited on Easter morning if I have observed Lent. One year I tried not observing Lent on purpose since I currently attend a church that does not observe it. When Easter came, it felt like any other Sunday, only more crowded.

It lacked the specialness that it usually holds for me. I encourage you to try to observe Lent in order to fully appreciate Easter.

One breakfast tradition our family enjoys is making empty tomb rolls. These are crescent rolls that have marshmallows baked in them to represent Jesus's body. When they are fully cooked, the marshmallows melt, thereby leaving an empty tomb.

While our family does not make a big deal out of Easter baskets, I know that many people do. If you do like to make baskets, I would encourage you to add something to the basket that would further your child's spiritual walk with the Lord. This may be a new a book that you think they would like that has a Christian message, or a biblically based coloring book, or something else that would strengthen their walk with the Lord. Of course, you know your child best.

If you are looking for a craft to do on Easter, try constructing a Resurrection garden. There are plenty of tutorials online. These small gardens use a half-buried pot or can as an empty tomb with grass or moss planted on top of it and around it. Then decorate as you choose with things such as rocks, crosses, and flowers. Many of the items you probably have around the house.

RESOURCES

Bergren, Lisa Tawn. *God Gave Us Easter*. Colorado Springs: WaterBrook, 2013. This book is part of the *God Gave Us* series. It is a gentle book that talks about the significance of Easter by using a family of bears talking about why they are celebrating. It does incorporate the Easter bunny, so if you do not like that, skip this one.

Denney, Christy. "Empty Tomb Rolls." *The Girl Who Ate Everything*. https://www.the-girl-who-ate-everything.com/empty-tomb-rolls/. This has a simple recipe for empty tomb rolls.

Gordon, Beth. "Resurrection Garden—Easter Activity for Families." *123Homeschool for Me*. https://www.123homeschool4me.com/our-easter-resurrection-garden_26/. Here is one of the many sites to get started on a Resurrection garden. Note, many would say that you might want to start this a week earlier, or even on Good Friday.

Laferton, Carl. *The Garden, the Curtain, and the Cross (Tales that Tell the Truth)*. Charlotte: The Good Book Company, 2016. This book gives a wonderful Gospel description. The pictures are vibrant, and it shows the theological significance of what Jesus did through the rending of the veil. This is probably my favorite Easter book for kids.

Mackall, Dandi Daley. *Journey, Easter Journey*. Nashville: Tommy Nelson, 2004. This is a rhyming story about Jesus. Mackall recalls how Jesus came to earth and then how he died. The pictures are very well done.

"Resurrection Eggs." *Bible Games Central*. https://biblegamescentral.com/resurrection-eggs/. Resurrection Eggs are a tactile way to tell the Easter story. Each egg has a small item depicting a part of the death and resurrection of Jesus. You can either purchase a set, or this website instructs on how to make your own with a corresponding script.

THE EASTER SEASON

Easter is not a one-day event in the church calendar, but rather seven weeks. The new reality that Jesus creates by his death and resurrection takes some time to discover and explore. It gives us a chance as believers to understand how this makes an impact on our lives. Let us give ourselves permission to do something fun with our families these weeks. Spending time outside with your family is an easy way to do this, especially as the weather usually turns nicer around this time. Go for family walks or hikes, or merely plan a picnic at a local park or playground. Make desserts that you normally would only make for "special occasions," or maybe plan family game nights once a week. Perhaps there is something that your family really enjoys, but you find that you keep putting it off. Takes these weeks to make it a priority. Whatever you do, it should be fun.

For daily time in the Word, I would suggest doing an in-depth study on the book of Acts with your kids if they are old enough. Luke records some amazing stories of God's signs and wonders. *Kids Read Truth* has an Acts book for tweens. Studying one of the Gospels is another good option.

Below I offer some activities much like I did for Lent, but not as exhaustive. I think after the intensity of Lent, sometimes we need to breathe a little. By this point in your journey into the church year, you have probably started to figure out what does and does not work with your kids. Some kids really like crafts, and others prefer activities. Some kids even really like to just get into studying the Word. As with Ordinary Time, this can be a time of experimenting with new ways to seek after God. Here are some suggestions to get your creative juices flowing.

Week 1: The Road to Emmaus, Luke 24:13–35

Jesus walks with some of his followers after his resurrection, but they only recognize him after he breaks bread. It reminds us of a number of things. One, that we often do not see the full picture of what Jesus is doing until he makes himself known. His followers knew him, and discussed all that had happened, but Jesus illuminates for them a deeper understanding of his death. Two, Jesus walks with us, even when we do not see him or recognize him. Jesus is alive even though we do not see him now.

Suggested Memory Verse: Luke 24:32

Suggested Activities

After reading the story you can remind your children that Jesus is always with us. Create pictures with your footprints and write, "Walk with Jesus." Reinforce the idea that we need to walk with Jesus each and every day. We decide to follow him, and he desires to be in relationship with each of us. Our feet are individual and special, and Jesus wants to walk with us because he loves each of us.

Play this game with your kids. Blindfold one of the kids or send them out of the room. Next, move or change something in the room. When the child returns, let her try to guess what has been changed. We need to be aware of not only our physical surroundings, but also our spiritual ones as well. We pray that Jesus will open our eyes to see what he is doing in our world.

For a fun treat make pitas with hummus, since this is a Middle Eastern food. Reiterate that when Jesus sat down to eat with his followers and he broke the bread, their eyes were opened.

Week 2: Jesus Appearing to the Disciples, John 20:19–31

Jesus appears to his disciples after his resurrection. This passage starts with Jesus breathing on them and giving them his peace. It then transitions to the doubting Thomas story. While many people pay particular attention to Thomas, since we all doubt at times, Jesus bestowing his peace forms the heart of the passage. It is more powerful to underscore how Jesus gives us peace. It is only in Jesus that we are made whole and new. It is only in Jesus that we can find proof to combat our doubts, because Jesus is the only one who can truly speak peace into our lives.

Suggested Memory Verse: John 20:21

Suggested Activities

Jesus gives his peace by breathing on his disciples. Teach your children some breathing exercises. This can be as simple as taking ten slow deep breaths to calm themselves down. Experiment with your kids about breathing. Have them walk around your house once and see how they are breathing. Then have them run around once and now see how they are breathing. We need more oxygen when we work harder. When we try to do things without Jesus' peace, it is like running all the time; we have to work harder. When we invite Jesus in and his peace, it is easier to breathe.

Make a stress ball from a balloon and flour to help bring peace. Simply fill an uninflated balloon with some flour and knot it. I suggest using a funnel and doing this outside because it is messy. When your children feel stressed and not at peace, have them squeeze their stress ball.

My kids love to color, so I printed a simple coloring page that said PEACE that I found on the internet. You could also just write the word peace on a sheet of paper and ask how we define it. Let your kids color and talk about what it means to have peace.

Week 3: New Life in Jesus, 1 Corinthians 15:35–58

Here Paul talks about the new life we find in Jesus. Last week we recognized that only through Jesus can we find peace and wholeness, now this week we acknowledge only in Jesus can we find that all things have been made new. We have been made into a new creation by Jesus' life, death, and resurrection. This can be a hard concept to grasp for little kids. Even though kids may not understand how we need to be made new, they can understand how some days are just bad, and how they wish they could start the day all over and make different choices. They understand how out of dead things new things can grow by looking at nature, such as a new tree growing out of a dead stump.

Suggested Memory Verse: 1 Cor 15:44b

Suggested Activities

Observing nature lends itself to understanding new life. As mentioned, new trees sprout out of dead stumps, so go on a nature hike and try to find new life out of old. Grow plants in a garden. Wrap a bean seed in a wet paper towel and place it in a plastic bag. This way your children can see how the shoot comes out of the dead seed and is a totally new thing.

Animals also exhibit new life. Butterflies come from caterpillars, but it is still the same insect, only changed. It has a new life after spending time in a chrysalis. Here is a link to a bunch of caterpillar and butterfly crafts at *B-Inspired Mom*, https://b-inspiredmama.com/caterpillar-and-butterfly-crafts/. Spend one day on caterpillars and how they act, and then another day making butterfly crafts to illustrate new life. Find videos online that show this process, and then relate it to our lives in Jesus: we become a completely new creature in him, with new abilities and new opportunities, but we are still the same person, new and old all at the same time. The process is not always easy, nor does it usually happen overnight, but it is worth it.

Week 4: Jesus as the Good Shepherd, John 10:1–18

Jesus describes himself as the good shepherd in John 10. We may or may not like being called sheep, since I am sure we have all heard sermons on how stubborn sheep are. We need guidance, and we need Jesus to be our shepherd. While acknowledging we are wandering sheep, Jesus as the shepherd shapes the passage. Jesus calls himself the gate. He will protect his sheep; and he has already laid down his life for us. What is required of us is to follow.

Suggested Memory Verse: Psalm 23:1

Suggested Activities

Sheep centered crafts work well for this week. One of the best sites I have found is *Ministry to Children* at https://ministry-to-children.com/the-good-shepherd-crafts/. It has not only a small teaching on John 10, but also three crafts that you can easily do at home. I also appreciate how the focus is not merely on sheep, but rather on Jesus, who is the shepherd for the sheep. Our teaching should always point back to Jesus.

Week 5: Jesus is the Way, John 14:1–14

Jesus covers a lot of ground in this passage, from stating he is going ahead to make a place for his followers; to declaring he is the Way, the Truth, and the Life; and finally, if anyone has seen Jesus, then that person has seen the Father. Do your children need to hear that Jesus has a plan for them? You may want to reinforce to them that Jesus is preparing a place. If your child is struggling with discipline and following Jesus, then Jesus as the Way might be where you want to start. Jesus shows us that he is more than we can ever truly imagine. He shows us who he is in so many ways, because we need so many reminders of who he is!

Suggested Memory Verse: John 14:6

Suggested Activities

Use building blocks or Legos and build a house together, or draw a picture of your child's dream house. Describe all the rooms in the house, and how Jesus creates the best houses.

For Jesus as the Way, I really like the website *Ministry to Children.* They have many ideas for this week at https://ministry-to-children.com/jesus-is-the-way-craft-ideas/. She suggests making a map or a treasure hunt. The kids need to find the right way to the treasure. If you can't do that, create an obstacle course with tape on the floor. This is one of my kids' favorite activities, and we reuse this idea throughout our Bible time when we need to work on following directions.

Go on a nature hike for Jesus is the Life. Look for all kinds of life, such as birds, squirrels, plants, trees. Make a scavenger hunt for them to see how many living things they can find. Remind your children that Jesus made the earth and gives us all life.

Pull together some family photographs and make a collage. When we look at ourselves and our parents and grandparents, we see resemblances. Talk about how knowing Jesus means we know the Father as well.

Week 6: Spreading the Good News, Acts 17:16–33

As disciples of Jesus, we are called to tell others about him, and to teach them to grow in his ways. As parents, we are called to do this first and foremost with our children. For our children, this may be a hard concept. I remember when I was six, I had a conversation with my mom about why some people don't believe in Jesus. I couldn't understand what was so hard about it, and why everyone in the world didn't believe in him. God's existence was obvious to me. I have had similar conversations with my own kids. How to tell others about Jesus can be tricky, so working with your children when they are young to be winsome and truth tellers is helpful.

As we read the book of Acts, we see that the disciples took advantage of what was going on around them. Many times they went into the synagogues and taught. Other times, such as when Paul preaches at Mars Hill, the citizens asked him to present his teaching. Sometimes the apostles performed miracles in order to show people the power of Jesus. The same strategies hold true for us today. Sometimes we may give in-depth teaching, sometimes we form relationships with people, and sometimes we pray for miracles.

Suggested Memory Verse: Matthew 28:19–20

Suggested Activities

Being able to share how God has made an impact in your life not only reminds you of the God's faithfulness, but sets the groundwork for skeptical people to see how a loving God desires a relationship with them. Have your children tell a story about something God did in their lives. Illustrate and write the story down so they have a tangible reminder of the goodness of God.

Ask your children why they believe in Jesus. Work through with them the reasons why so they are ready in season and out of season to be ambassadors of Christ.

Week 7: God will protect, Acts 12:1–19 and Acts 16:16–40

It is hard to live in this world sometimes, and God can feel far away. Our kids may ask, does God answers our prayers? Here God moves in a mighty way to protect his people from prison. In Acts 12:1-19, and in Acts 16:16-40, God frees Peter, and Paul and Silas respectively from prison. In Peter's story, he goes to where the people are praying for him, and in Paul and Silas's case, they stay and evangelize to the guard. In both accounts, God provided a way where there was no way. He freed his believers from jail, and he protected them. We as Christians are not immune to hardship as these stories prove, but God walks with us through the hardship.

Suggested Memory Verse: Acts 16:31

Suggested Activities

These are similar passages, so you can look at one passage, or perhaps read one passage on one day of the week, and then follow it up with the second one later on in the week. Since in both incidents believers were put in chains, make a paper chain. Write different things on each link, such as a word from the memory verse, different prayer requests, or names of people who have told your children about Jesus.

Highlight that people prayed for Peter's release. In fact, once he is freed, he goes to where they are holding a prayer meeting. Talk about the power of prayer, and the power of faith. It may feel at times that God will not answer our prayers, but he does. Take this opportunity to pray for something and watch for how God answers. Start a prayer journal with your kids by writing down specific prayer requests and then how they are answered. Make a prayer jar. Place craft sticks with prayer requests written on them. Every day you can pull a different one to pray about. Once it is answered, take it out of the jar.

Construct a jail out of blocks and then have it fall down to simulate the earthquake. Draw a picture of the disciples in prison with popsicle sticks over the picture to represent the bars. Then free the disciples by pulling away the bars.

7

Ascension and Pentecost

ASCENSION, HISTORY AND THEOLOGY

Ascension takes place forty days after Easter and is the day that we celebrate Jesus returning to heaven. Jesus spent forty days teaching and ministering after he rose from the dead. He strengthened and encouraged the disciples to be prepared for the upcoming missionary life. His disciples enjoyed a few more days with their beloved teacher, and Jesus enlightened them on how to understand God better. Then, Jesus went back to God the Father to sit at his right hand and to be king. He is now our intercessor. While Pentecost ushers in a new reality with the Holy Spirit, Ascension first acknowledges Jesus sitting on the throne once again in heaven. Since this always takes place on a Thursday, many churches choose to celebrate it on the following Sunday.

As a holy day, it seems to have been a late arrival to the calendar, but there are some indications that it was celebrated in Jerusalem by the mid-fourth century. Easter originally encompassed all the aspects of today's separate feasts. In other words, Easter celebrated Jesus's resurrection, his ascension, and the coming of the Holy Spirit. We see that the church started to spread out these days to coincide with the biblical timeline, in that Jesus stayed for forty days, and Pentecost coincides with the Jewish Pentecost fifty days after Easter.

HOW CAN I GET STARTED?

Since this is a holiday that celebrates an event that took place out-side on a mountain, it is traditional to go for a hike, so get out-side with your family! Go for a hike or a walk. Play at a park or playground. Take along a picnic and enjoy being outside together. Pack a simple meal for the picnic and bring along a fun dessert that somehow evokes clouds. I also like to make a nice dinner for my family. My family does not particularly like things like meringues that would evoke clouds, so for dessert we usually have some sort of white dessert, like cake with white icing, or cookies with icing. Choose whatever would be fun for your family.

RESOURCES

Baden, Robert. *Jesus Returns to Heaven (revised) Easter Arch Books.* St. Louis: Concordia, 2003. As with other Arch books, this short book tells the story of Jesus' ascension in sweet rhymes and is nicely illustrated.

Castle, Becky. "Jesus' Ascension to Heaven Emergent Reader." *Teachers Pay Teachers.* https://www.teacherspayteachers.com /Product/Jesus-Ascension-to-Heaven-Emergent-Reader-Distance-Learning-5362165?msclkid=8af843e6f5141a941af7 23f9941a851a&utm_source=bing&utm_medium=cpc&utm_ campaign=Shopping%20-%20All%20Products%20-%20 Desktop%20%7C%20US-%20%243.00%20USD%20-7.99%20 USD&utm_term=4574999167580096&utm_content=All%20 Products. This is a cheap printable book you can download from Teachers Pay Teachers. It goes over the basics, and your child can color it.

Gordon, Beth. "Jesus Ascends bile Craft for Kids." *123 Homeschool 4 Me.* https://www.123homeschool4me.com/jesus-ascends-bible-craft-for-kids_4/. Here is a simple fun craft we have done. It shows Jesus ascending by using a plastic cup.

PENTECOST, HISTORY AND THEOLOGY

Pentecost is the church's birthday. It celebrates the coming of the Holy Spirit to empower and equip the saints in spreading the Gospel. The book of Acts recounts how the disciples were praying in a room when tongues of fire appeared on their heads, and how the Holy Spirit gifted them in speaking different languages. Peter preached a sermon which brought thousands into the church. The disciples, no longer afraid and cowering in a room, boldly declared that Jesus is the Messiah. They are given the power of the Holy Spirit to preach and perform miracles in Jesus' name for the glory of God. Many in the early church saw this as a sealing of the New Covenant, since the Jewish feast of Pentecost celebrated the giving of the Law and the Old Covenant.

Pentecost took place on the Jewish holiday of Shavuot, which is a Celebration of Weeks. As one of the three feasts God required his people to celebrate in Jerusalem, it explains why so many people were in Jerusalem when the Holy Spirit came. The term Pentecost comes from the Greek word denoting the fiftieth day from Passover. It is traditionally a dairy heavy holiday for Jews. Kosher laws dictate that meat and dairy do not mix at meals; therefore, some meals have meat, and some have dairy. Cows and other milk producing animals go through a dry spell for part of the year. Pentecost coincided with the return of the milk, so it is typically a feast that features cheesy dishes and fish. These include things like cheesecake, kugel, and salmon.

As a Christian holiday, we have some suggestions that it was celebrated as early as the second century, and definitely by the middle of the third. It celebrates several things. First, as previously mentioned, it is the cementing of the New Covenant. Second, it proclaims the unity we find in the church. We are all brought together to live a new life. As such, it also commemorates baptism, and for those in the Pentecostal tradition, the baptism of the Holy Spirit especially. Finally, although we are united, there is still great diversity in the body of Christ. As Paul reminds us in First Corinthians, there is one body, but many parts. We must all work together with the various gifts God has given us for the church to function well. Many churches treat Pentecost as a major holiday. Some read the Scriptures in different languages to exemplify what the original Pentecost must have felt like. Others may throw a birthday party for the church. Still others may not observe it much at all, and if that is the case where you are, then you may want to do something special for the day.

HOW CAN I GET STARTED?

Pentecost is the holiday that ends the Easter Season, and is the last big holiday before the Advent Season. So, enjoy it! As the birthday of the church, you may want to throw a party, or at least have a birthday cake. Traditionally people wear red on the day to signify the coming of the baptism of fire by the Holy Spirit.

If you want to feature special foods for your day, you might want to choose dairy foods—macaroni and cheese, cheesecake, ice cream, cream sauces for anything, really. This honors the Jewish roots of the holiday and allows you to make it distinctive. My kids are not cheesecake eaters, but they love macaroni and cheese and ice cream.

Pentecost integrates several different themes: the flame, the wind, and the dove. If you choose to use the fire of the Holy Spirit resting upon the disciples, include flames and fire in your day. Eat spicy foods to evoke the fire of the Holy Spirit. Decorate a cake with flames and fire. For a craft, cut out headbands with flames attached to them.

If you choose to emphasize the wind, you can have a lot of fun making crafts such as kites, windsocks, or pinwheels. I have to admit, when we have tried to make pinwheels in the past, they have been less than successful. Some kites have fared better than others, and of course you need a windy day for any of these to work at all. You can also simply make paper airplanes and have fun trying to make them fly in the wind. If you are really fancy, decorate them with wind related themes or even dove related themes. Make paper fans. Another angle you may choose to take with the wind is to re-member how the disciples spoke in different tongues. Take time to learn some phrases in another language or listen to a Bible passage in different languages.

Finally, the dove is not only a sign of peace, but also a symbol of the Holy Spirit. Research doves on the computer or a library book. Keep a look out for them around your house, or any other bird as well. Below there is a link to a paper plate bird craft. If your kids are older and up for a challenge, try your hand at folding origami birds.

RESOURCES

Currie, Jackie. "Paper Plate Birds." *Happy Hooligans Art Craft Play.* https://happyhooligans.ca/paper-plate-birds/Here is the link to find the paper plate bird craft. It is super easy and fun to decorate as the kids wish.

Hutto, Rebekah McLeod. *The Day When God Made Church: A Child's First Book About Pentecost.* Brewster, MA: Paraclete, 2016. This is a very colorful book, and my younger children enjoyed reading this. It gives a broader understanding of Pentecost than the Arch Book does.

Jaeger, Elizabeth. *The Pentecost Story (Arch Books).* Saint Louis, MO: Concordia, 2013. This is a short book that gives the story of Babel, and how this is rectified through Pentecost. It is in the form of a rhyming poem. My older daughter liked this book.

"Pentecost Messy Church Crafts." *Flame: Creative Children's Ministry.* http://flamecreativekids.blogspot.com/2013/05/pentecost-messy-church-crafts.html. This children's ministry has some good ideas for Pentecost crafts. They do messy church, which is a ministry focused on giving children a hands-on experience to church. Their website also has lots of other ideas for different times of the year, as well as children's ministry.

'Stained Glass Craft." *DLTK's Crafts for Kids.* http://www.dltk-bible.com/crafts/m-stainedglass.htm. *DLTK's* website, which has a lot of different craft ideas for all sorts of things, also has a stained-glass window craft if your children are more into cutting and pasting.

"How to Make Origami Birds." *WikiHow*. https://www.wikihow. com/Make-Origami-Birds. Here are step-by-step instructions on how to make origami birds.

8

Reformation Day, All Saints Day, and Christ the King

The season after Pentecost is again Ordinary Time. This is summer through November. As I stated with Epiphany, this is a prime time to dig into books of the Bible, do devotionals that you enjoy, etc. Refer back to the Season after Epiphany for ideas. There are three holidays that I would like to highlight: Reformation Day, All Saints Day, and Christ the King.

REFORMATION DAY, HISTORY AND THEOLOGY

Reformation Day celebrates the day Martin Luther nailed his 95 Theses to the Wittenberg church door. It is heralded as the action that sparked the Reformation leading to today's Protestant churches. While the 95 Theses deal primarily with the issue of indulgences, official church documents that allowed the payer to shave time off their stay in purgatory, it nonetheless started a new movement. As more people realized they could read the Bible for themselves and hear God speaking to them in a new way, the Roman Church lost its influence in some areas. The Reformation allowed for the laity to become more involved in the church.

HOW CAN I GET STARTED?

Reformation Day happens to fall on Halloween. I do think observing Reformation Day is a better way of to celebrate the day than Halloween. Halloween may seem innocuous enough, but its occultic roots are apparent. My husband and I both remember dressing up for Halloween, but as we learned more about what it celebrates, we became convicted that this was not something honoring God. People dress up in order to confuse demons. For those who follow the pagan calendar, this is Samhain: a day when the veil between the living and the dead is much thinner. We need to ask ourselves if this is what we want to do with our time and worship? In our family we hand out candy in order to be good neighbors and to show love to the kids around us, but it is the one day I do not let my kids wear dress up, and we do not go trick or treating. I tell them about Martin Luther and the steps he took to reform the church. This is a major event both historically and ecclesiastically.

RESOURCES

Maier, Paul L. *Martin Luther. A Man Who Changed the World*. St. Louis: Concordia, 2004. This book has detailed pictures and tells the story of Martin Luther for kids.

ALL SAINTS DAY, HISTORY AND THEOLOGY

The day after Reformation Day is All Saints Day. Many Protestants shy away from this day because it focuses on the "saints." But guess what, we are all saints! Yes, some people separate All Saints Day and All Souls Day, but we can just celebrate All Saints Day on 1 November. For those in the Roman tradition, it is a time to celebrate saints who do not have their own day on the calendar. It can be much more than that. We honor all those who have run the race before us. It is a day to remember how God uses people to further his kingdom.

Christians as early as the second century commemorated the martyrs of the faith typically on the day of their death. The early martyrs presented clear examples of what it meant to give one's life for Christ, and how to lead a fearless life. Pope Gregory III dedicated a chapel in St. Peter's in Rome to all the saints on 1 November during the 730s. This became an annual event, and henceforth all the saints who do not have their own feast day are celebrated on 1 November in the Catholic Church. Again, it is a time to thank God for the men and women he has placed before us to guide us in our walk with Jesus.

HOW CAN I GET STARTED?

If you have lost a loved one in the past year, this opens the possibility for a special remembrance. Recall how this person walked with the Lord and teach your children about his or her witness. By remembering we ease the grieving process. I know that each of the big days, birthdays, anniversaries, holidays, etc. are especially hard the first year. This is a day that the church as a whole recognizes that we lose saints here on earth to be with our Father in heaven. So, if you have lost someone, spend some time remembering that person.

If you have not lost someone in the past year, or you do not feel the need to remember one person in particular, celebrate all those saints that have run their race before us and have laid the path for us to know the Lord. Tell a story about someone who told you about Jesus, or how you became a Christian. Read stories about famous missionaries. Remember those missionaries who are currently serving the Lord, and perhaps spend extra time in prayer for them. I admit that I make my kids listen to one of my favorite hymns on that day: "For All the Saints Who from Their Labors Rest" by William W. How. It is a little long, but it tells how the people before us have lived righteous lives and are examples of how we too should live our lives to God.

RESOURCES

Chandler, Lauren. *Goodbye to Goodbyes (Tales that Tell the Truth)*. Charlotte: The Good Book Company, 2019. This is the story of Lazarus, and how Jesus raised him from the dead. As with all the books in this series, it is beautifully illustrated and tells the story in a fresh and wonderful way. Chandler brings out that Jesus does not want us to die, and that saying goodbye is hard. I think this is an appropriate book for All Saints Day.

CHRIST THE KING. HISTORY AND THEOLOGY

The final holiday of the church year is Christ the King. This is celebrated the Sunday before the first Sunday in Advent. We remember that Jesus is King. He does and will reign over all things. So even when things seem dark and there is no way through, Jesus is making a way. There is a solemnity of Christ the King, recognizing that at the end of the world, all will bow before Jesus, whether they served him during this life or not. He will not be denied his throne.

This is a new holiday, only instituted in 1925 by Pope Pius XI. He did it in the face of growing atheism and communism, hoping that people would not compartmentalize their lives. While the world was moving toward greater secularization, Pope Pius wanted the church to understand that Jesus is the true king of the universe. When it started, the holiday was celebrated at the end of October, but Pope Paul VI in 1969 moved it to its current position in the year as the last Sunday before Advent.

As a new holiday, I can understand people's reticence in celebrating it, however, I think that it is a powerful reminder that our true allegiance lies not in our nation, but in our King Jesus. As I write this, we are in the middle of the COVID-19 pandemic. Governments around the world are scrambling trying to make the best decisions. We see more and more cases every day. We do not seem to have the power over this disease, and to be honest, we don't. Many people are looking to blame someone, and of course politicians are using this as a chance to play political games. We can get fed up with it. This holiday is a helpful reminder that Jesus is ultimately on the throne. Even though our current governments make mistakes, and we feel powerless to make a real difference, Jesus is the King of the universe. He holds the whole world in his hands.

HOW CAN I GET STARTED?

This holiday usually falls around Thanksgiving, so it is a festive time of the year already. Celebrating can be as easy as making crowns for the kids and having them decorate them. By doing this, you will want to explain that Jesus is the true King, the King of all kings, and yet he calls us friends and brothers and sisters. We gain inheritance in his kingdom, and as such we gain crowns as well. Jesus is still the High King.

Some cultures have a King Cake similar to what might be served on Epiphany or Mardi Gras as well. Again, because this is a relatively new holiday, I think that making your own traditions will be the most meaningful. My kids do not especially like King cakes, so we might have a different cake, or a special dessert. I try to make something special for them for the day.

Show your children a picture of an icon named Christ Pantokrator, which means Christ all powerful or ruler of all. It has many variations, but it shows that Jesus is the King of the world, and it is very beautiful.

RESOURCES

McCandless, Jake and Tyson Ranes. *Jesus and His White Horse*. Rapid City, SD: Crosslink, 2020. This book is brightly illustrated and deals with how Jesus will return to set all things right and be our true king.

Conclusion

I hope that this book has given you some ideas about how to incorporate faith into your lives in a new way. My prayer is that you are able to include a few things this year, and then a few more next year to give shape to your family's life. As I said in the introduction, this is not to make you feel guilty for not doing some things, but rather to give you more tools in your toolbox as parents to bring faith alive to your family. Please do not feel the need to do everything. Seek God in what he would have you do with your family. I know I still struggle with what to do sometimes with my kids, but if I have a framework, I find that it is easier. Each day my prayer for my family is that God will help me to raise them for what he wants them to do. My prayer is that you grow deeper in your relationship with Jesus through each year.

Remember, you know your kids best, and you know what they need. Some of what I have suggested may seem a bit silly, but try it any way. I am always surprised when something I thought was a bit ridiculous really worked with my kids. As the parents, we set the tone. If you have not had family Bible time with your family, it may feel a little weird to start, but do it anyway. There are days I do not know what to say. There are days I feel like my kids are not getting it, or it feels forced. Keep trying, keep plugging away at it because as parents we have the responsibility to lead our children. Keep seeking God on what you should do, and how you should do it.

Finally, I offer one last piece of advice for finding other resources. The ones I have included in this book meet certain criteria. I look for Bible based books and websites that support good doctrine. When you have exhausted these resources and are looking for more, keep your doctrinal radar out. Check to see who publishes the material. If it is from a denomination that does not hold the same core doctrines you do, then keep looking. Some of the resources included give lists of other resources, so use them as a starting place. You can do this.

Remember, the almighty God who created the whole earth eagerly awaits spending time with you and your children. He will guide and nurture your relationship if you let him. This is merely a tool in your toolbox, and as with any tool, it is only useful when used at the right time in the right place. My prayer is it supports you in your walk with Jesus.

Bibliography

Danielou, Jean. *The Bible and the Liturgy*. South Bend: University of Notre Dame Press, 1956.

Forbes, Bruce David. *America's Favorite Holidays: Candid Histories*. Oakland, CA: University of California Press, 2015.

———. *Christmas: A Candid History*. Berkeley: University of California Press, 2007.

Gross, Bobby. *Living the Christian Year: Time to Inhabit the Story of God*. Downers Grove, IL: IVP, 2009.

Hedahl, Susan K. *Proclamation and Celebration: Preaching on Christmas, Easter, and Other Festivals*. Minneapolis: Augsburg Fortress 2012.

Warren, Tish Harrison. *Liturgy of the Ordinary: Sacred Practices in Everyday Life*. Downers Grove, IL: IVP Books, 2016.

Webber, Robert E. *Worship is a Verb: Eight Principles for Transforming Worship*. Peabody, Mass: Hendrickson, Inc., 1997.